Numeracy Focus

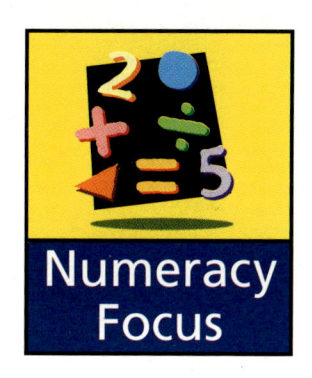

Class Focus Book 4

Mike Askew • Sheila Ebbutt

RIGBY

10 × 10 tables grid

×	1	2	3	4	5	6	7	8	9	10
1	1	2	3	4	5	6	7	8	9	10
2	2	4	6	8	10	12	14	16	18	20
3	3	6	9	12	15	18	21	24	27	30
4	4	8	12	16	20	24	28	32	36	40
5	5	10	15	20	25	30	35	40	45	50
6	6	12	18	24	30	36	42	48	54	60
7	7	14	21	28	35	42	49	56	63	70
8	8	16	24	32	40	48	56	64	72	80
9	9	18	27	36	45	54	63	72	81	90
10	10	20	30	40	50	60	70	80	90	100

1–100 grid

1	2	3	4	5	6	7	8	9	10
11	12	13	14	15	16	17	18	19	20
21	22	23	24	25	26	27	28	29	30
31	32	33	34	35	36	37	38	39	40
41	42	43	44	45	46	47	48	49	50
51	52	53	54	55	56	57	58	59	60
61	62	63	64	65	66	67	68	69	70
71	72	73	74	75	76	77	78	79	80
81	82	83	84	85	86	87	88	89	90
91	92	93	94	95	96	97	98	99	100

Place value grid

1000	2000	3000	4000	5000	6000	7000	8000	9000
100	200	300	400	500	600	700	800	900
10	20	30	40	50	60	70	80	90
1	2	3	4	5	6	7	8	9

1a

- four thousand
- two hundred
- seventy
- one thousand
- eight hundred
- fifty
- six
- three
- seven thousand
- twenty
- nine
- five hundred

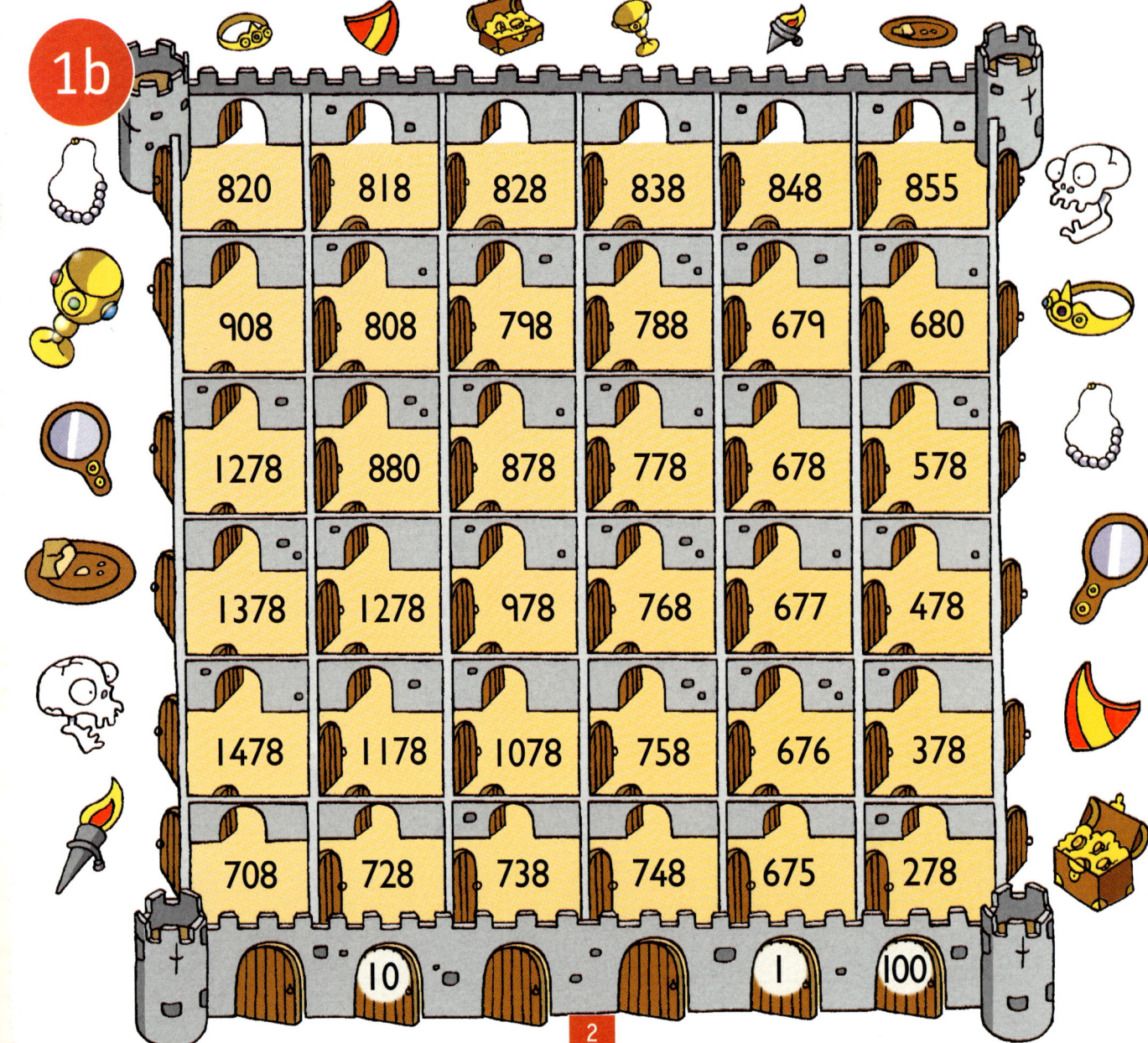

1b

820	818	828	838	848	855
908	808	798	788	679	680
1278	880	878	778	678	578
1378	1278	978	768	677	478
1478	1178	1078	758	676	378
708	728	738	748	675	278

10   1   100

1c

2a **A**

8
2
3
9
5
1
12
4
7
13
10
6
11

B

❶ 7 + 15

❷ 18 + 5

❸ 8 + 13

❹ 9 + 17

❺ 16 + 6

4

2b Ⓐ

Stones: 60, 20, 30, 10, 40, 90, 50, 80, 70

Ⓑ

90 − 40
500 + 300
160 − 90
800 + 700
1800 − 600

80 − 50
600 + 300
170 − 80
700 + 700
1600 − 800

2c

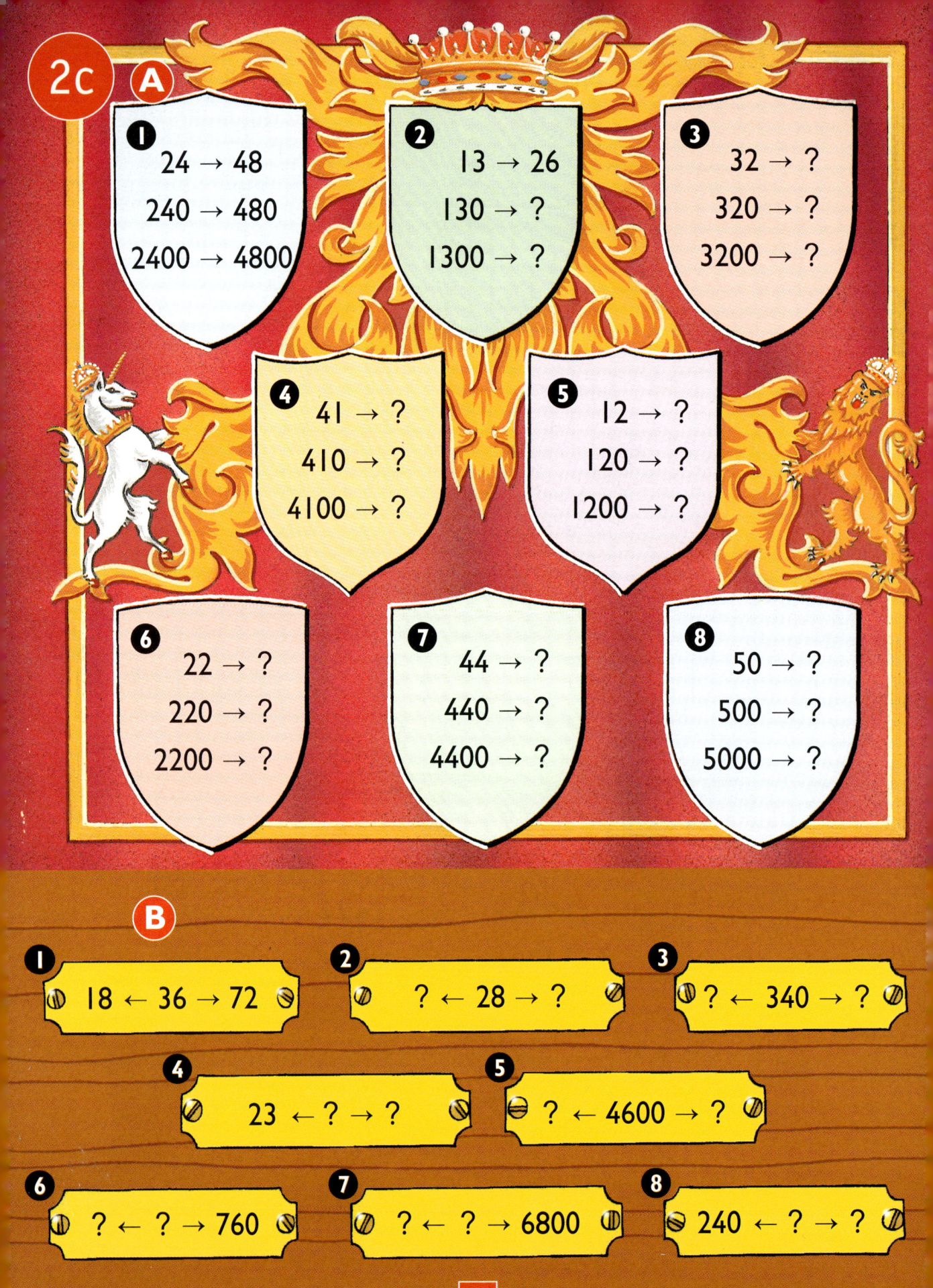

A

1.
24 → 48
240 → 480
2400 → 4800

2.
13 → 26
130 → ?
1300 → ?

3.
32 → ?
320 → ?
3200 → ?

4.
41 → ?
410 → ?
4100 → ?

5.
12 → ?
120 → ?
1200 → ?

6.
22 → ?
220 → ?
2200 → ?

7.
44 → ?
440 → ?
4400 → ?

8.
50 → ?
500 → ?
5000 → ?

B

1. 18 ← 36 → 72

2. ? ← 28 → ?

3. ? ← 340 → ?

4. 23 ← ? → ?

5. ? ← 4600 → ?

6. ? ← ? → 760

7. ? ← ? → 6800

8. 240 ← ? → ?

3a

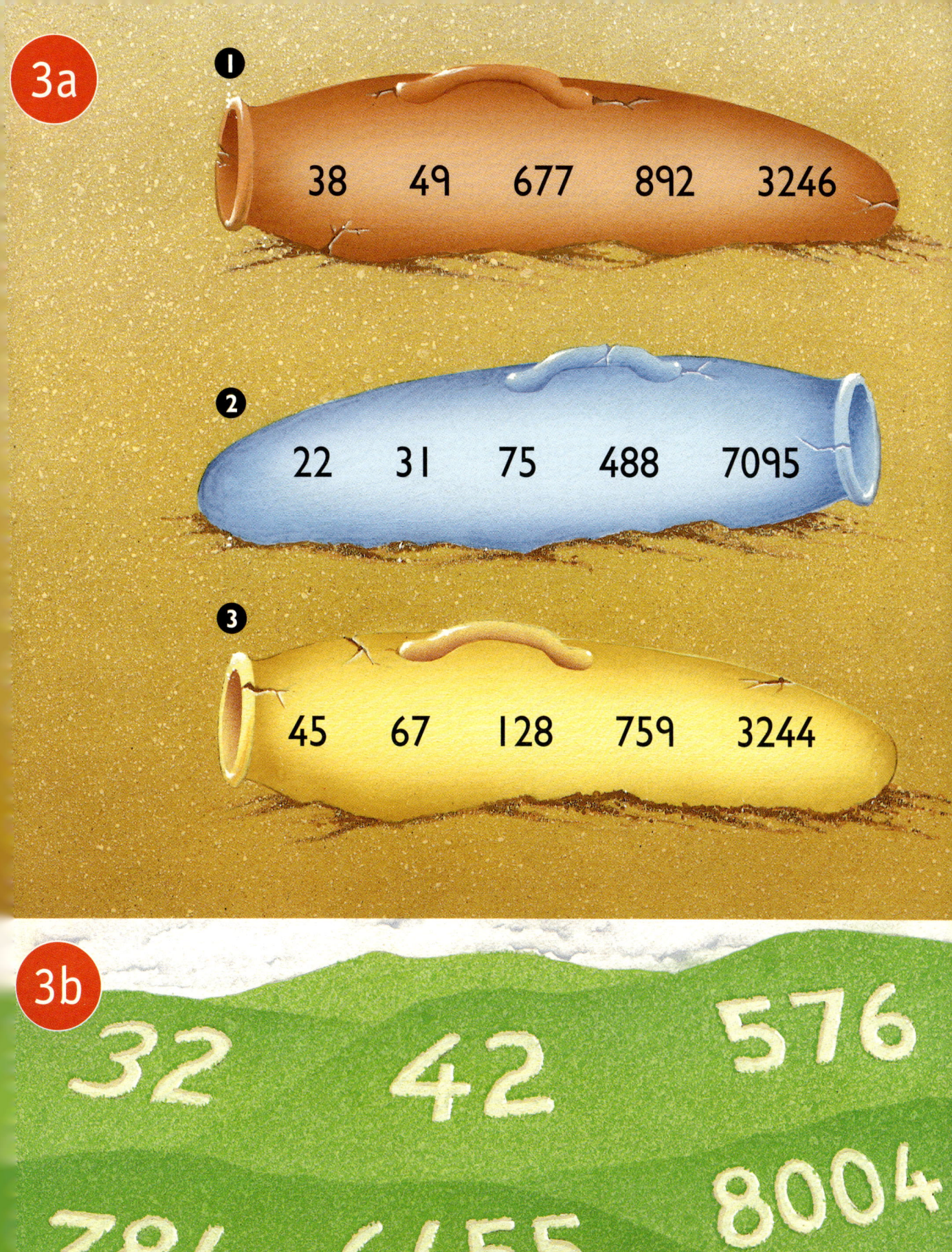

① 38   49   677   892   3246

② 22   31   75   488   7095

③ 45   67   128   759   3244

3b

32   42   576

781   6455   8004

3c

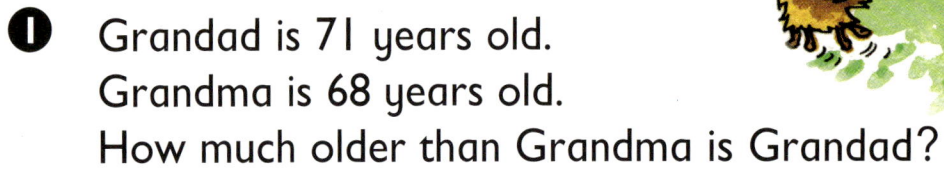

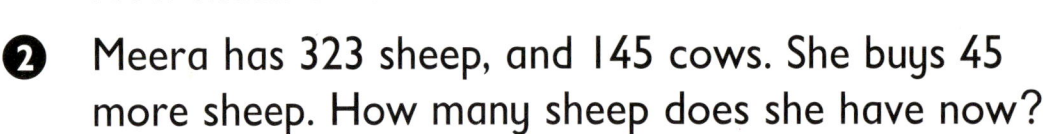

A

1. Grandad is 71 years old. Grandma is 68 years old. How much older than Grandma is Grandad?

2. Meera has 323 sheep, and 145 cows. She buys 45 more sheep. How many sheep does she have now?

3. Mount Kuma is 4002 metres high. Mount Hawk is 3997 metres high. How many metres taller is Mount Kuma than Mount Hawk?

4. For the Rovers match 5877 people arrived. Sixty people had to leave before the match started. How many stayed to see the match?

5. It is 403 km from Smallville to Gotham City. The Kent family have travelled 396 km from Smallville. How much further do they have to travel to reach Gotham City?

B

73 − 66

428 + 4

702 − 697

8649 + 2

4004 − 3996

92 − 87

238 + 5

504 − 498

6318 + 3

5002 − 4997

4a

4b

A

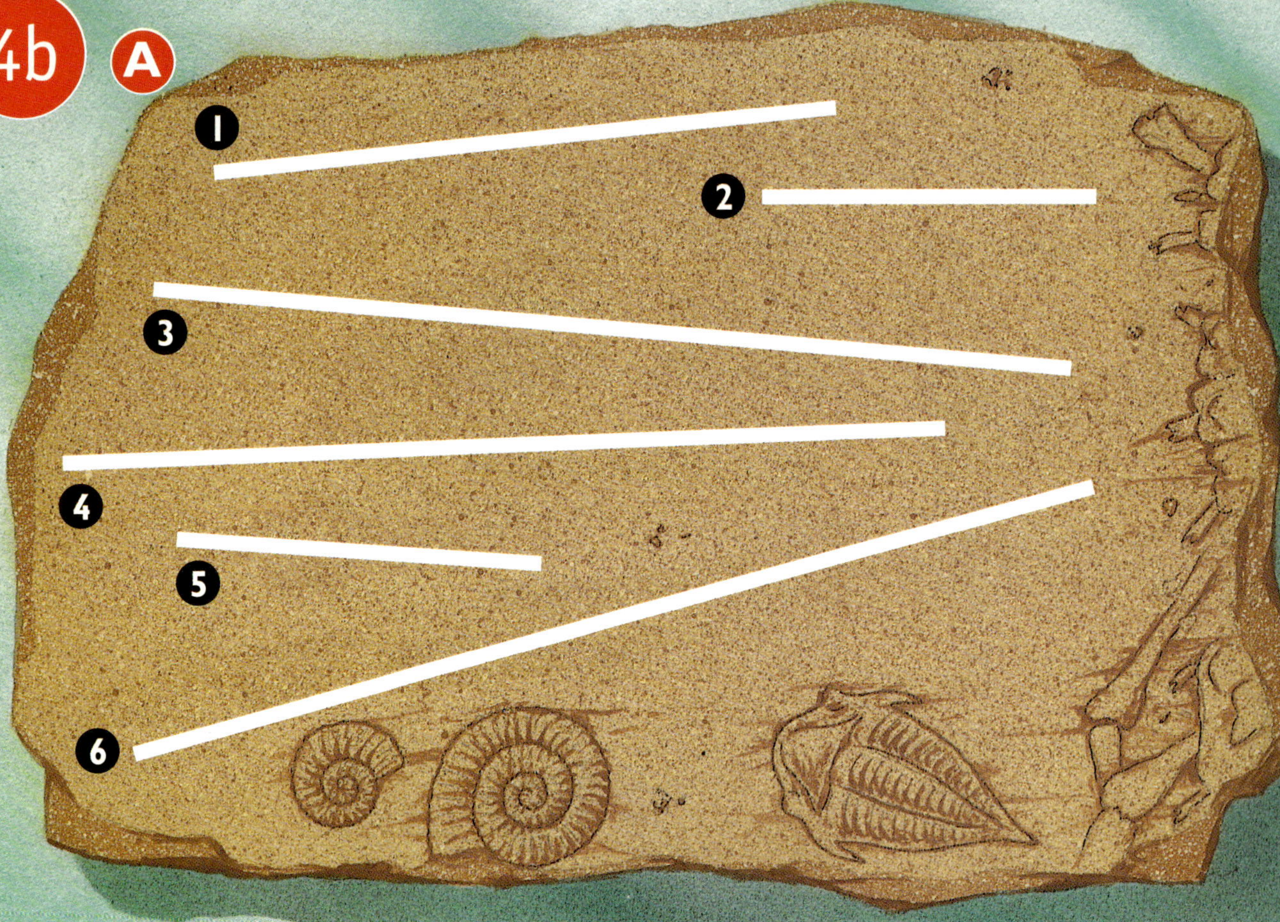

B

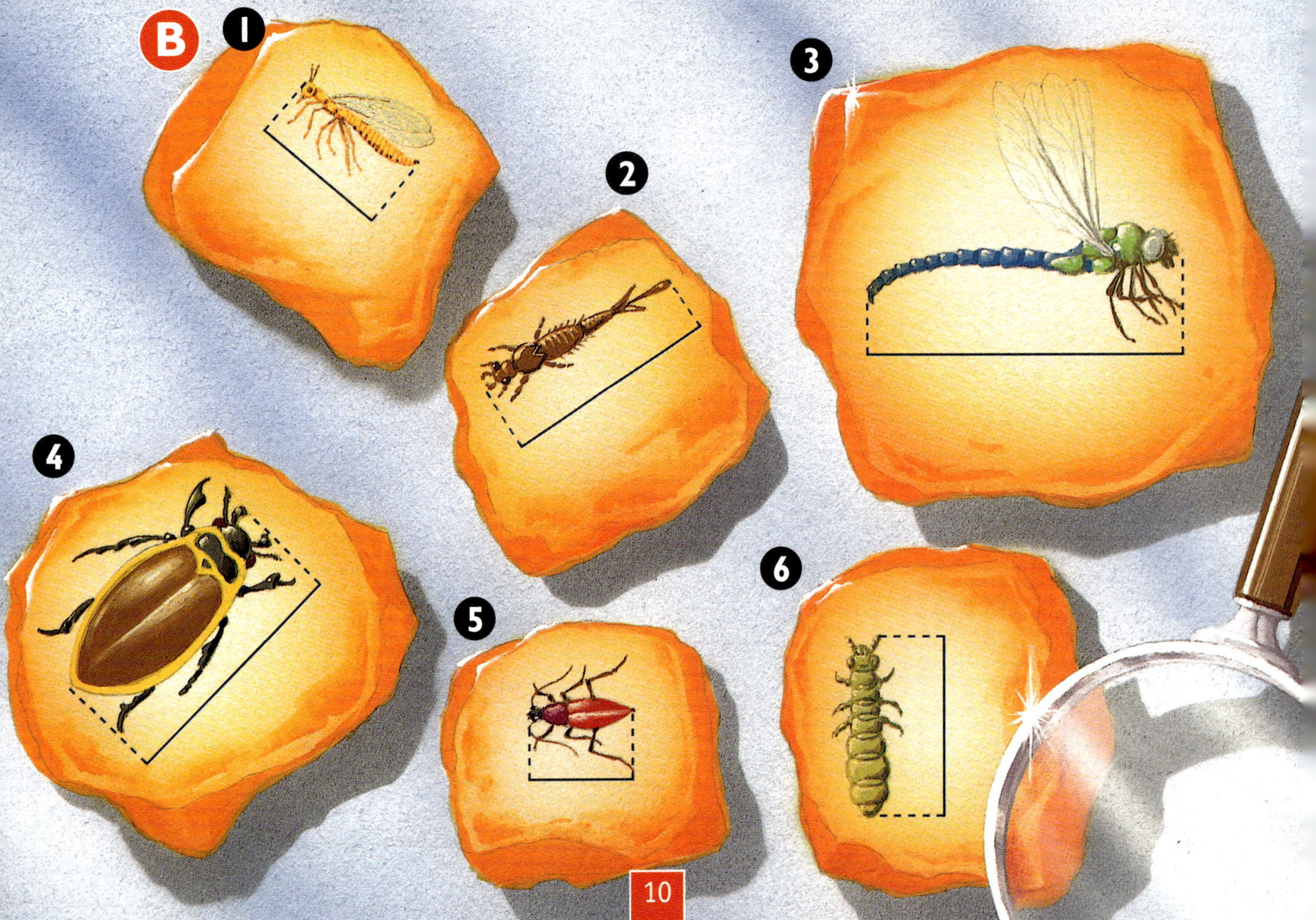

5a

5b

A

B

12

Iceland's Volcanoes

Mount Krafla is an old volcano. It first erupted 2300 years ago.
Last erupted: 1984

Öraefajökull lies beneath a huge glacier.
Last erupted: 1727

Mount Askja erupted violently in 1875, killing people and animals.
Last erupted: 1961

Grimsvötn is an active volcano.
Last erupted: 1998

Mount Hekla is Iceland's most active volcano.
Last erupted: 1991

Heimaey erupted in 1973, leaving a crack in the earth 2 kilometres wide.
Last erupted: 1973

Surtsey erupted in 1963, rising 130 metres from the seabed.
Last erupted: 1967

① How many years is it since Mount Krafla last erupted?

② How many years is it since Surtsey last erupted?

③ How many years were there between Mount Askja's last eruption and Mount Hekla's last eruption?

④ Could your great-grandmother have been alive when Mount Öraefajökull last erupted?

7a

sometimes   **always**   **never**

1. If you add an odd number and an even number you get an even number.
2. If you add two odd numbers you get an even number.
3. If you add two even numbers you get an even number.
4. If you add two even numbers you get an odd number.
5. If you add an odd number and an even number you get an odd number.
6. If you add two numbers bigger than a thousand you get an even number.
7. If you add two odd numbers you get an odd number.

7b

$3 + 4 + 2 = 9$
$3 + 6 + 8 = 17$

9, 1, 5, 7, 3, 4, 2, 8, 6

8a

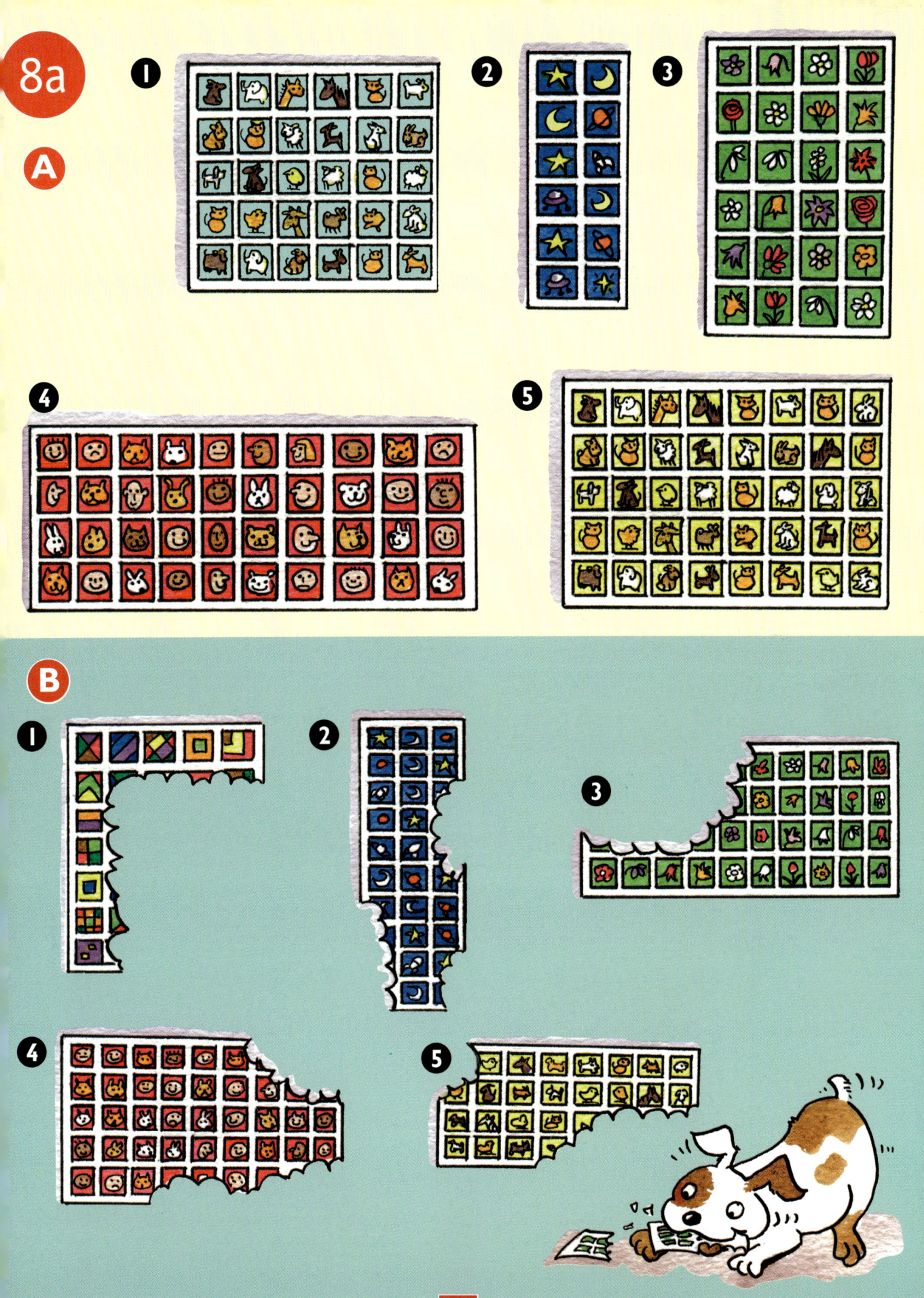

A

1
2
3
4
5

B

1
2
3
4
5

8b

1. double 35 = 70 | 35 × 2 = ☐ | 35 + 35 = ☐
2. double 36 = ☐ | 36 × 2 = ☐ | 36 + 36 = ☐
3. | 34 × 2 = ☐ |
4. | | 40 + 40 = ☐
5. double 39 = ☐ | |
6. | | 48 + 48 = ☐
7. | 26 × 2 = ☐ |
8. double 54 = ☐ | |

8c

1. 3 → 6 → 12   3 × 4 = 12
2. 6 → ☐ → ☐   6 × 4 = ☐
3. 4 → ☐ → ☐   4 × 4 = ☐
4. 8 → ☐ → ☐   8 × 4 = ☐
5. 7 → ☐ → ☐   7 × 4 = ☐
6. 12 → ☐ → ☐   12 × 4 = ☐
7. 23 → ☐ → ☐   23 × 4 = ☐
8. 18 → ☐ → ☐   18 × 4 = ☐
9. 25 → ☐ → ☐   25 × 4 = ☐

9a

1
double 23	
double 230	
double 2300	

2
double 41	
double 410	
double 4100	

3
double 37	
double 370	
double 3700	

4
double 32	
double 320	
double 3200	

5
double 28	
double 280	
double 2800	

6
double 49	
double 490	
double 4900	

9b   A

1. 3 → 30 → 15   3 × 5 = 15
2. 5 → ☐ → ☐   5 × 5 = ☐
3. 9 → ☐ → ☐   9 × 5 = ☐
4. 6 → ☐ → ☐   6 × 5 = ☐
5. 7 → ☐ → ☐   7 × 5 = ☐
6. 14 → ☐ → ☐   14 × 5 = ☐
7. 21 → ☐ → ☐   21 × 5 = ☐
8. 17 → ☐ → ☐   17 × 5 = ☐
9. 26 → ☐ → ☐   26 × 5 = ☐

9b

1. 4 → 40 → 80   4 × 20 = 80
2. 7 → ☐ → ☐   7 × 20 = ☐
3. 8 → ☐ → ☐   8 × 20 = ☐
4. 6 → ☐ → ☐   6 × 20 = ☐
5. 5 → ☐ → ☐   5 × 20 = ☐
6. 12 → ☐ → ☐   12 × 20 = ☐
7. 24 → ☐ → ☐   24 × 20 = ☐
8. 19 → ☐ → ☐   19 × 20 = ☐
9. 27 → ☐ → ☐   27 × 20 = ☐

9c

1. 2 × 3, area 6;   2 × 3 = 6
2. 3 × 4, area ?;   3 × 4 = ☐
3. 3 × ?, area 6;   3 × ☐ = 6
4. 4 × ?, area 12;   4 × ☐ = 12
5. ? × 3, area 9;   ☐ × 3 = 9
6. 3 × 5, area ?;   3 × 5 = ☐
7. 7 × ?, area 21;   7 × ☐ = 21
8. ? × 5, area 20;   ☐ × 5 = 20
9. 3 × ?, area 18;   3 × ☐ = 18

18

10a

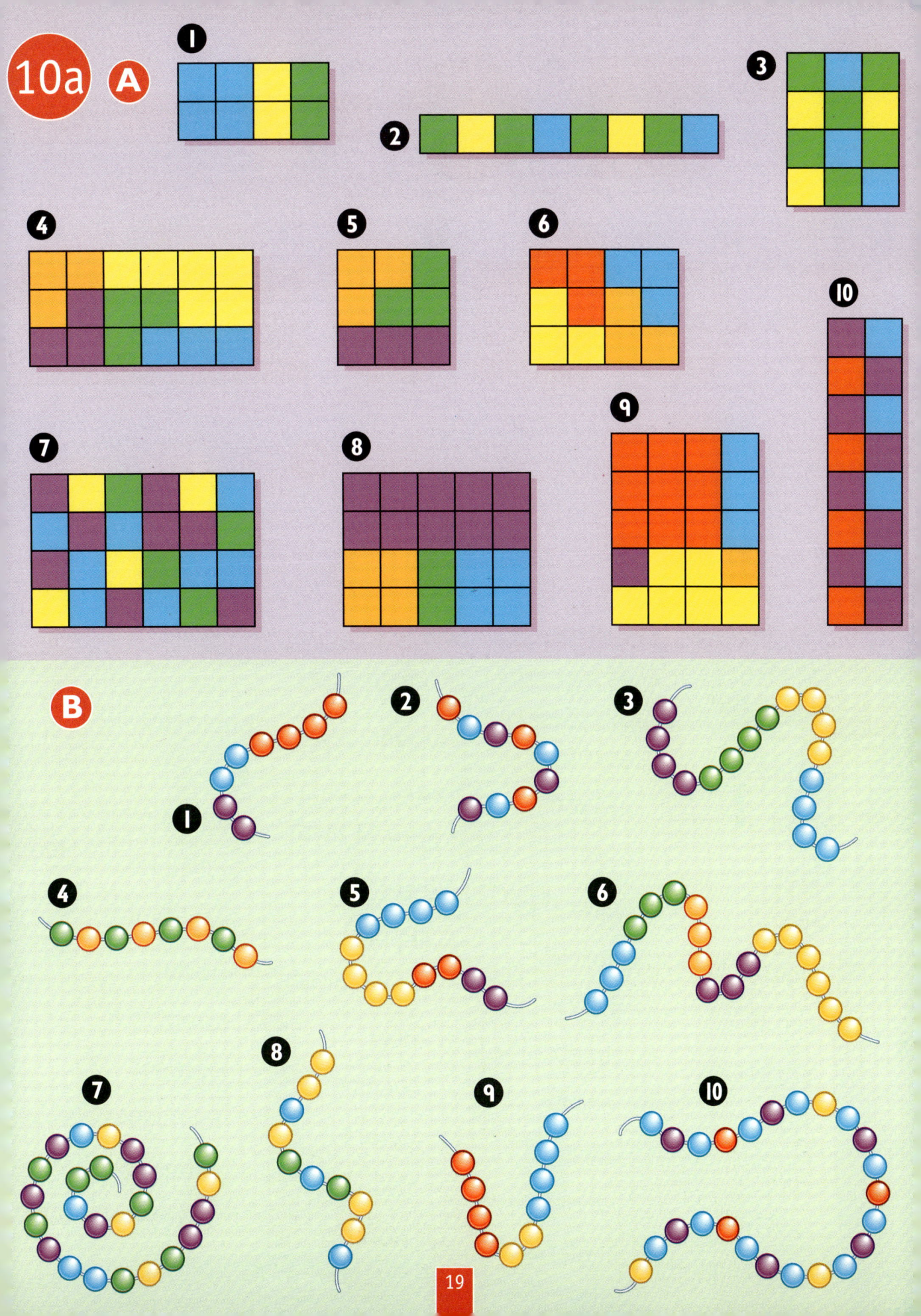

10b

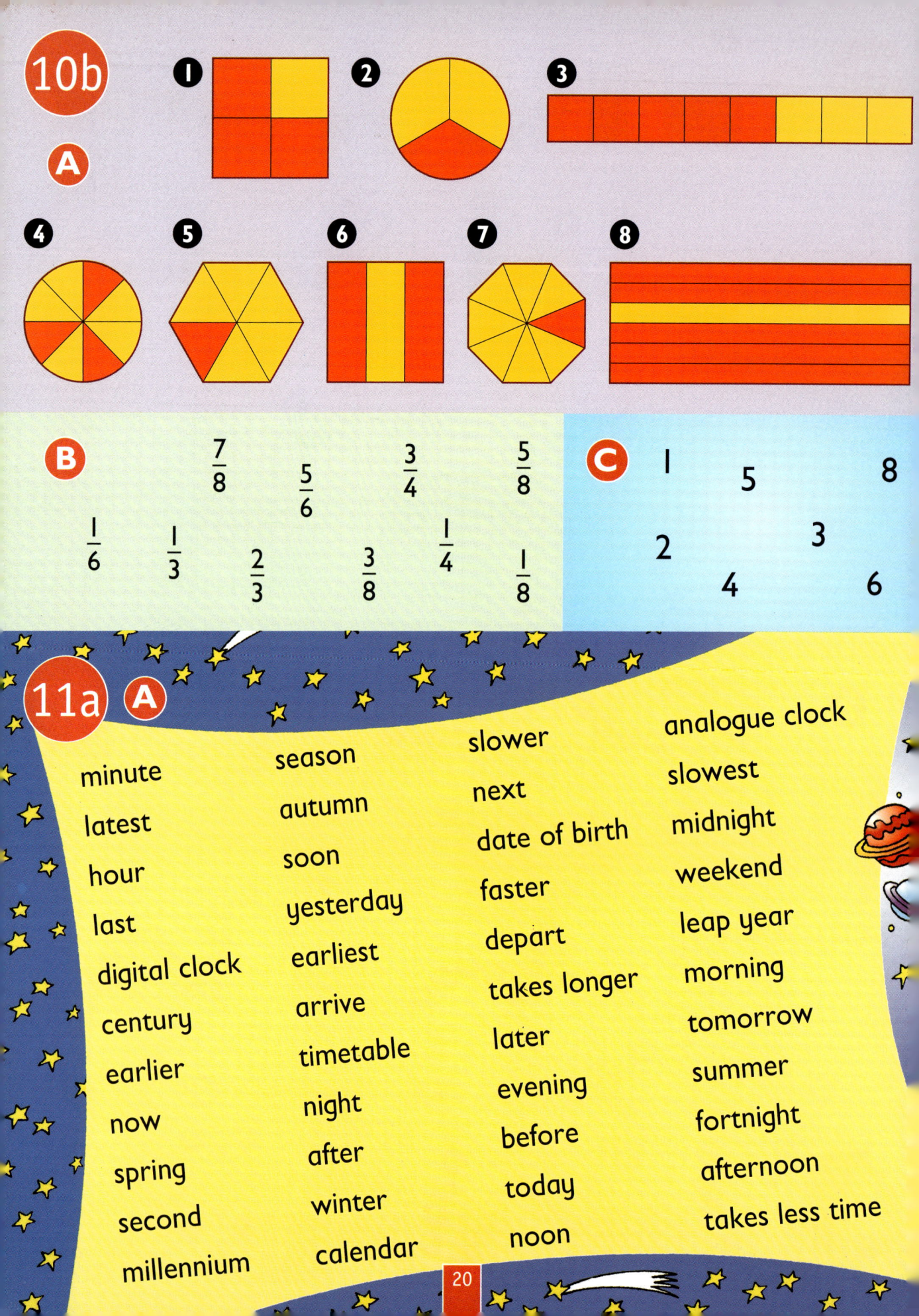

A

1.
2.
3.
4.
5.
6.
7.
8.

B

$\frac{7}{8}$ $\frac{5}{6}$ $\frac{3}{4}$ $\frac{5}{8}$

$\frac{1}{6}$ $\frac{1}{3}$ $\frac{2}{3}$ $\frac{3}{8}$ $\frac{1}{4}$ $\frac{1}{8}$

C

1   5   8
2   3
    4   6

11a

A

minute
latest
hour
last
digital clock
century
earlier
now
spring
second
millennium

season
autumn
soon
yesterday
earliest
arrive
timetable
night
after
winter
calendar

slower
next
date of birth
faster
depart
takes longer
later
evening
before
today
noon

analogue clock
slowest
midnight
weekend
leap year
morning
tomorrow
summer
fortnight
afternoon
takes less time

11a **B**

The time it takes to watch a film.

The time it takes to boil a kettle.

The time it takes to walk across the playground.

The time it takes for mustard and cress seeds to sprout.

about

2 hours

3 minutes

10 minutes

5 days

2 days

30 seconds

10 years

4 years

3 months

6 weeks

2 weeks

How long a school term lasts.

How long the school summer holidays last.

The time between each Olympic Games.

21

11b

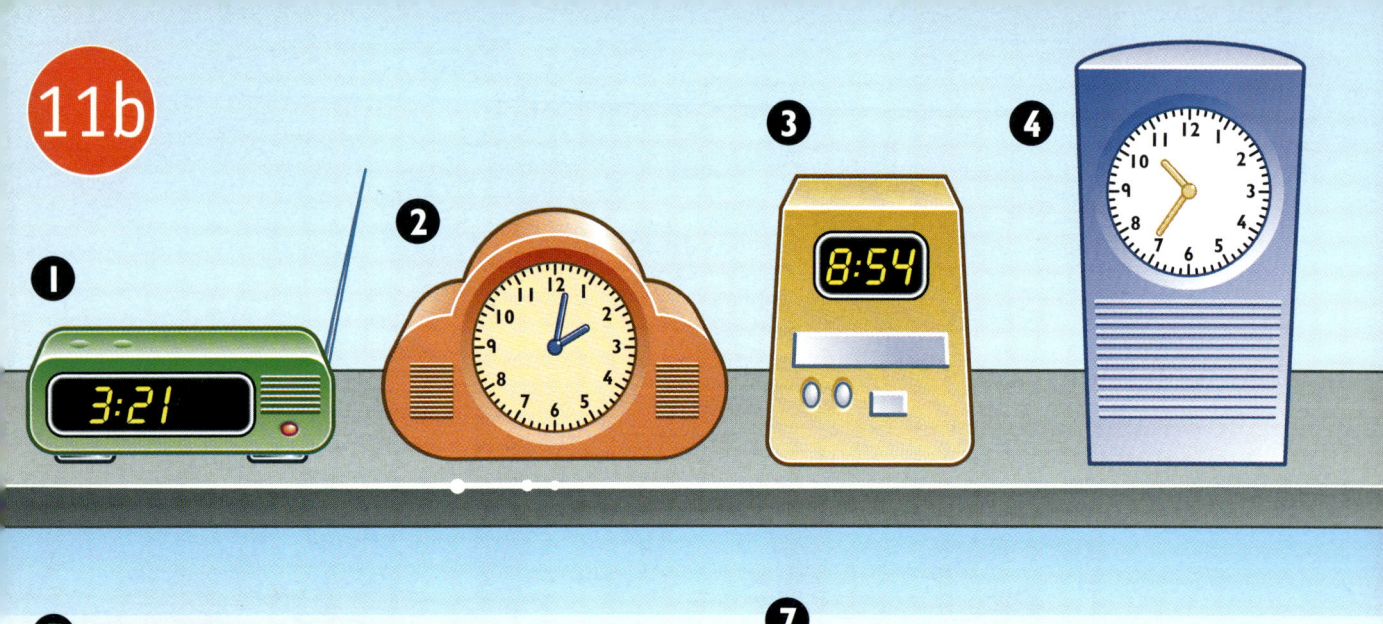

1. 3:21
2. (clock showing 12:00)
3. 8:54
4. (clock showing 7:00)
5. (clock showing 2:30)
6. 9:12
7. (clock showing 7:30)
8. 6:42

11c A

SHOWING TODAY

JURASSIC EARWIGS

Film lasts 1 hour 30 minutes

film starts	film ends
12:00	
1:45	
	5:00
5:15	

11c B

Wild West Theme Park

QUEUE HERE FOR WAGON TRAIN RIDE

Each ride takes 30 minutes

Annie's Pantry	Goldrush Creek		Fire Mountain		Annie's Pantry
departs	arrives	departs	arrives	departs	arrives
10:00 a.m.	10:05 a.m.	10:10 a.m.	10:20 a.m.	10:25 a.m.	10:30 a.m.
10:45 a.m.					
11:30 a.m.					
12:15 p.m.					

12 A

Amount of litter collected in one school week

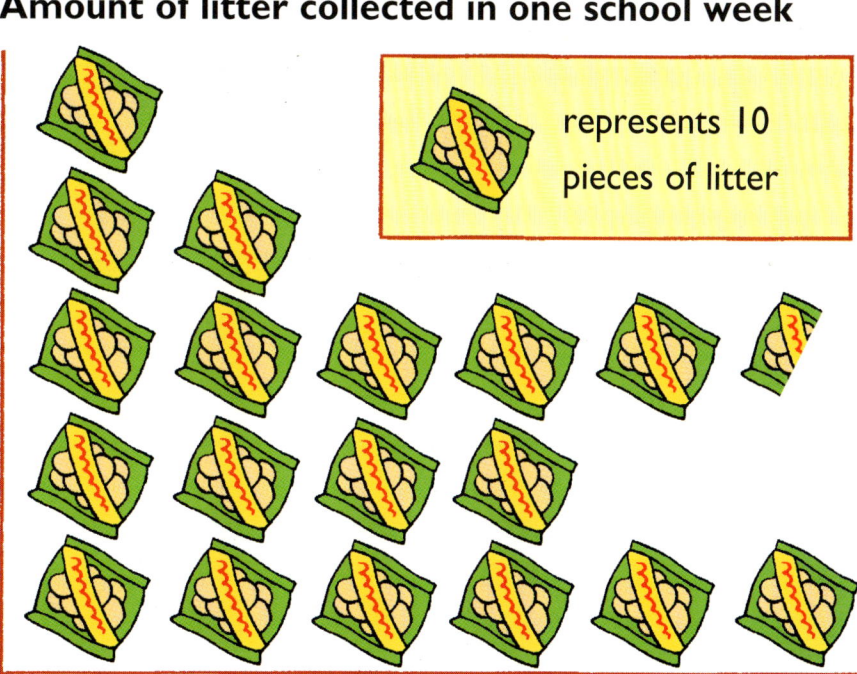

🌮 represents 10 pieces of litter

Day	Litter
Friday	🌮
Thursday	🌮🌮
Wednesday	🌮🌮🌮🌮🌮🌮🌮
Tuesday	🌮🌮🌮🌮🌮
Monday	🌮🌮🌮🌮🌮🌮

days of week

amount of litter

12 B

Rainfall at Halley Court School this week

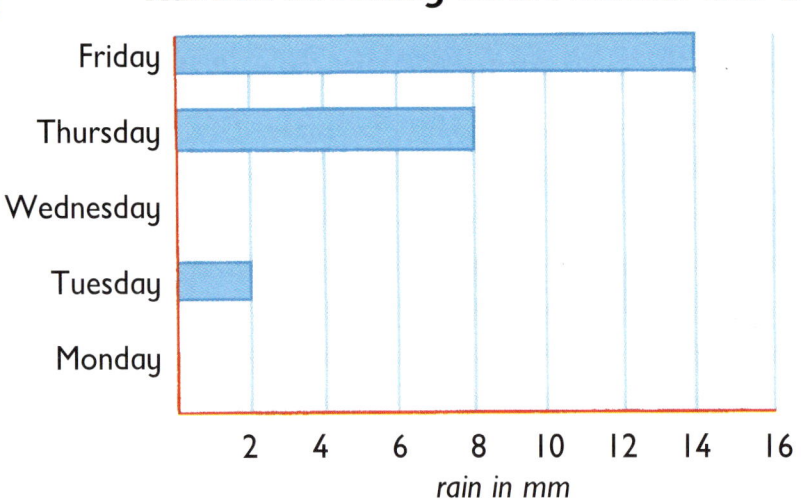

days of week	rain in mm
Friday	14
Thursday	8
Wednesday	0
Tuesday	2
Monday	0

Types of litter in school playground this week

	crisp packets	tissues	sweet papers	apple cores	drink cartons
Monday	𝍷𝍷𝍷𝍷 𝍷𝍷𝍷𝍷 𝍷𝍷𝍷𝍷 |||	𝍷𝍷𝍷𝍷 𝍷𝍷𝍷𝍷 ||	𝍷𝍷𝍷𝍷 𝍷𝍷𝍷𝍷 𝍷𝍷𝍷𝍷	𝍷𝍷𝍷𝍷	|||
Tuesday	𝍷𝍷𝍷𝍷 𝍷𝍷𝍷𝍷	𝍷𝍷𝍷𝍷	𝍷𝍷𝍷𝍷 𝍷𝍷𝍷𝍷 𝍷𝍷𝍷𝍷					
Wednesday	𝍷𝍷𝍷𝍷 𝍷𝍷𝍷𝍷 𝍷𝍷𝍷𝍷		𝍷𝍷𝍷𝍷		𝍷𝍷𝍷𝍷 𝍷𝍷𝍷𝍷 𝍷𝍷𝍷𝍷 𝍷𝍷𝍷𝍷			||	𝍷𝍷𝍷𝍷
Thursday	𝍷𝍷𝍷𝍷					𝍷𝍷𝍷𝍷 𝍷𝍷𝍷𝍷		
Friday							𝍷𝍷𝍷𝍷			

Amount of litter found on Monday

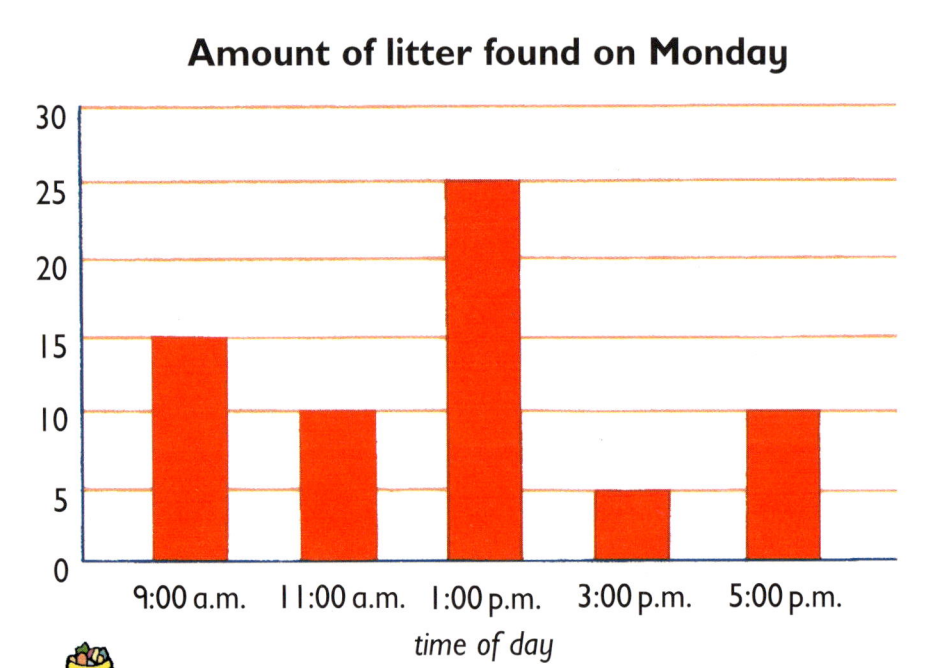

pieces of litter vs time of day:
- 9:00 a.m. — 15
- 11:00 a.m. — 10
- 1:00 p.m. — 25
- 3:00 p.m. — 5
- 5:00 p.m. — 10

13a

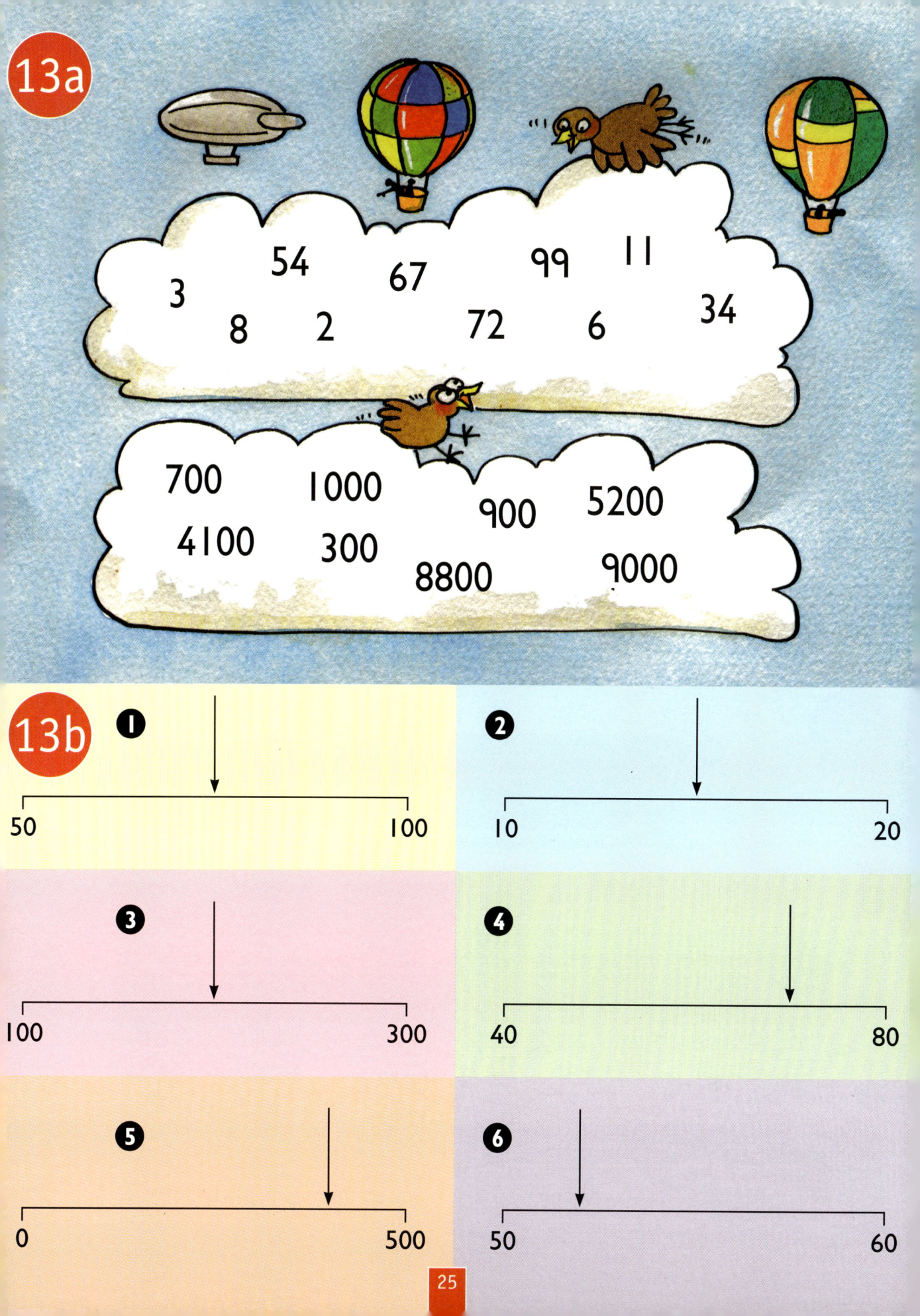

54   67   99   11
3   34
   8   2   72   6

700   1000
         900   5200
4100   300
         8800   9000

13b

1
50 ———↓——————— 100

2
10 ————↓—————— 20

3
100 ——↓———————— 300

4
40 —————↓———— 80

5
0 ————↓———— 500

6
50 ——↓————————— 60

13c

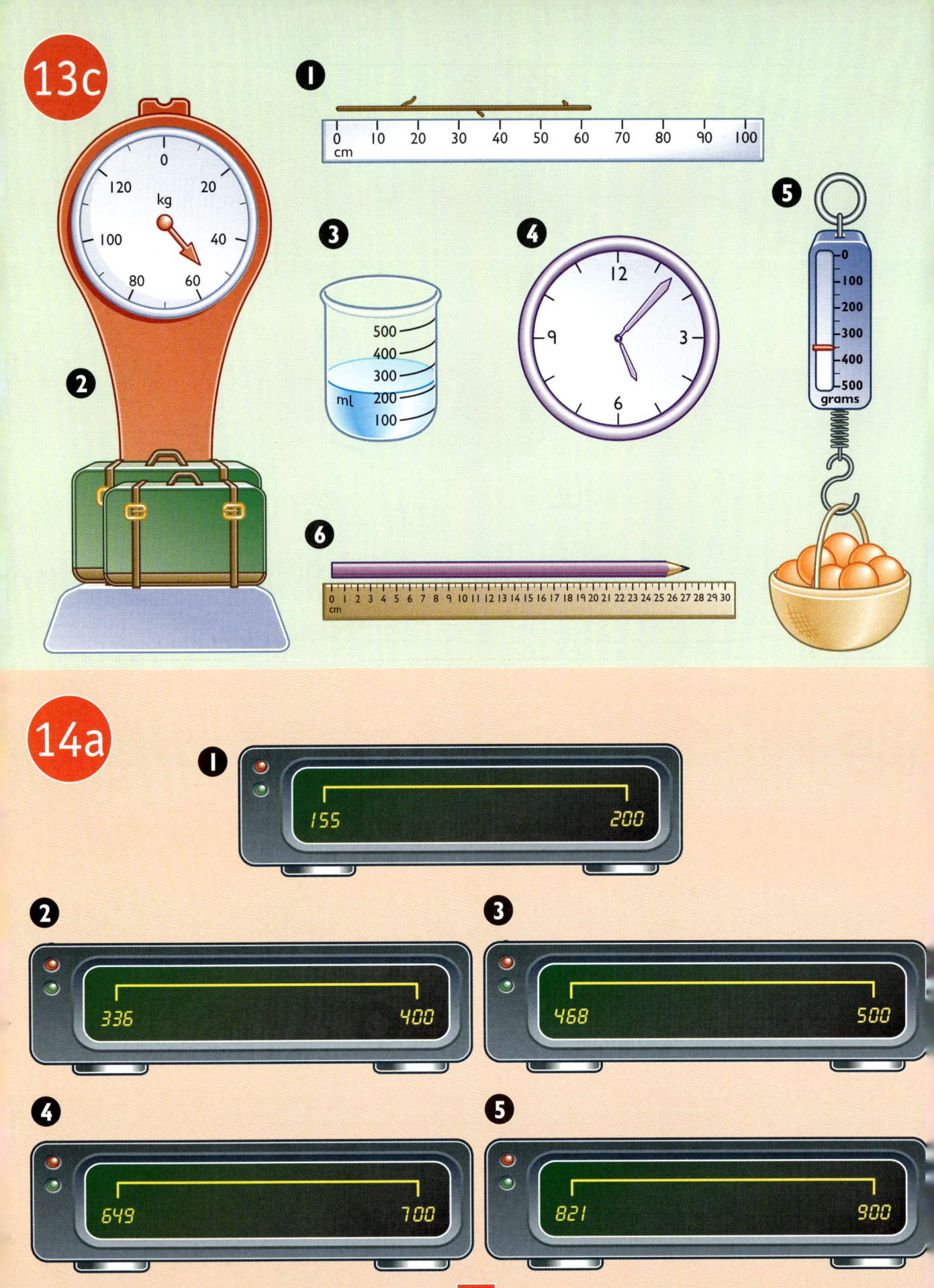

1.
2.
3.
4.
5.
6.

14a

1. 155 — 200
2. 336 — 400
3. 468 — 500
4. 649 — 700
5. 821 — 900

14b

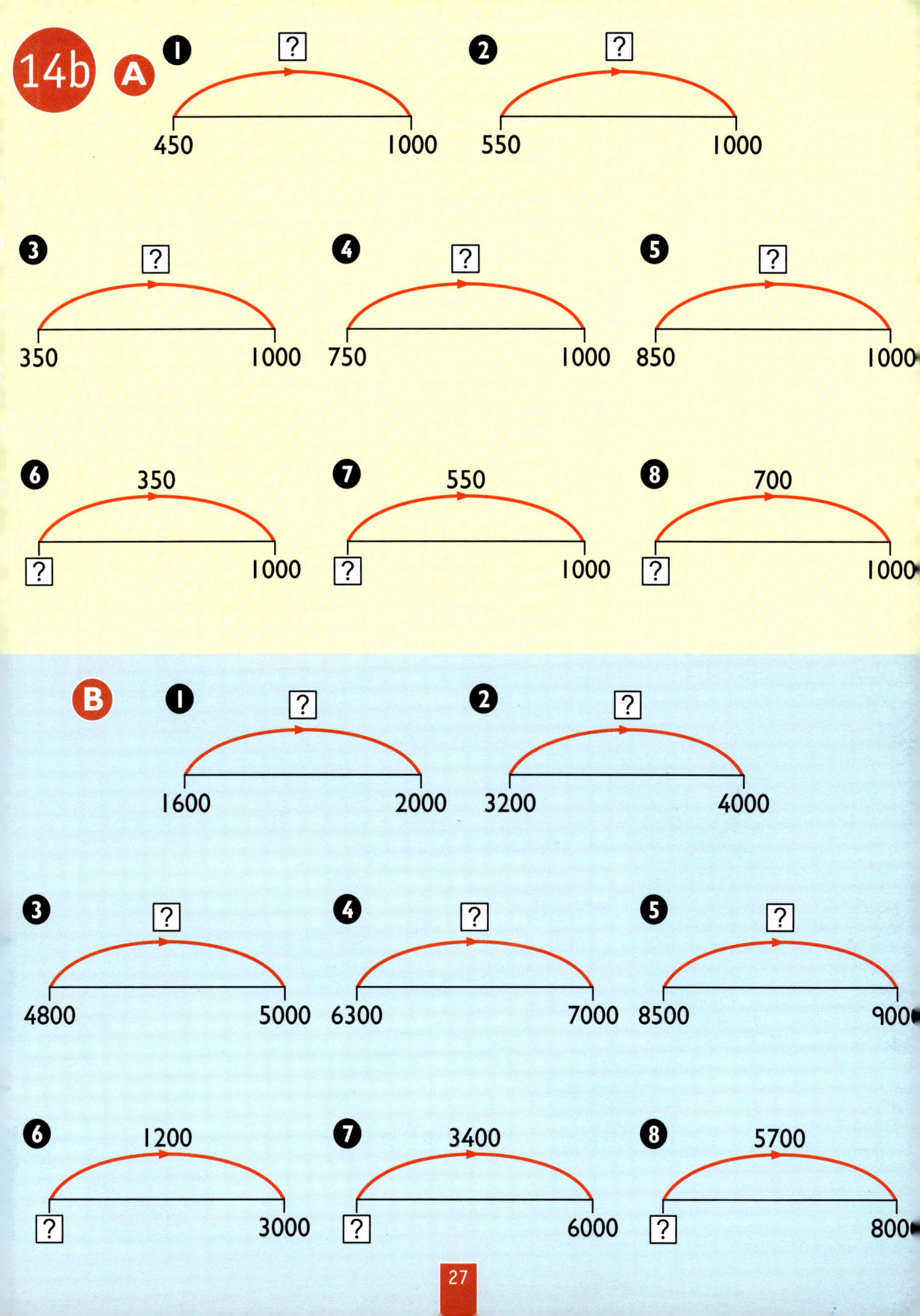

A

1 450 → ? → 1000

2 550 → ? → 1000

3 350 → ? → 1000

4 750 → ? → 1000

5 850 → ? → 1000

6 ? → 350 → 1000

7 ? → 550 → 1000

8 ? → 700 → 1000

B

1 1600 → ? → 2000

2 3200 → ? → 4000

3 4800 → ? → 5000

4 6300 → ? → 7000

5 8500 → ? → 9000

6 ? → 1200 → 3000

7 ? → 3400 → 6000

8 ? → 5700 → 8000

15a

1. 1 3 4 6 — 50
2. 1 1 4 6 — 30
3. 1 2 3 7 — 40
4. 1 2 3 8 — 50
5. 2 3 4 6 — 60
6. 2 3 4 7 — 70
7. 2 3 4 8 — 80
8. 1 3 5 9 — 90
9. 3 4 5 7 — 100

15b

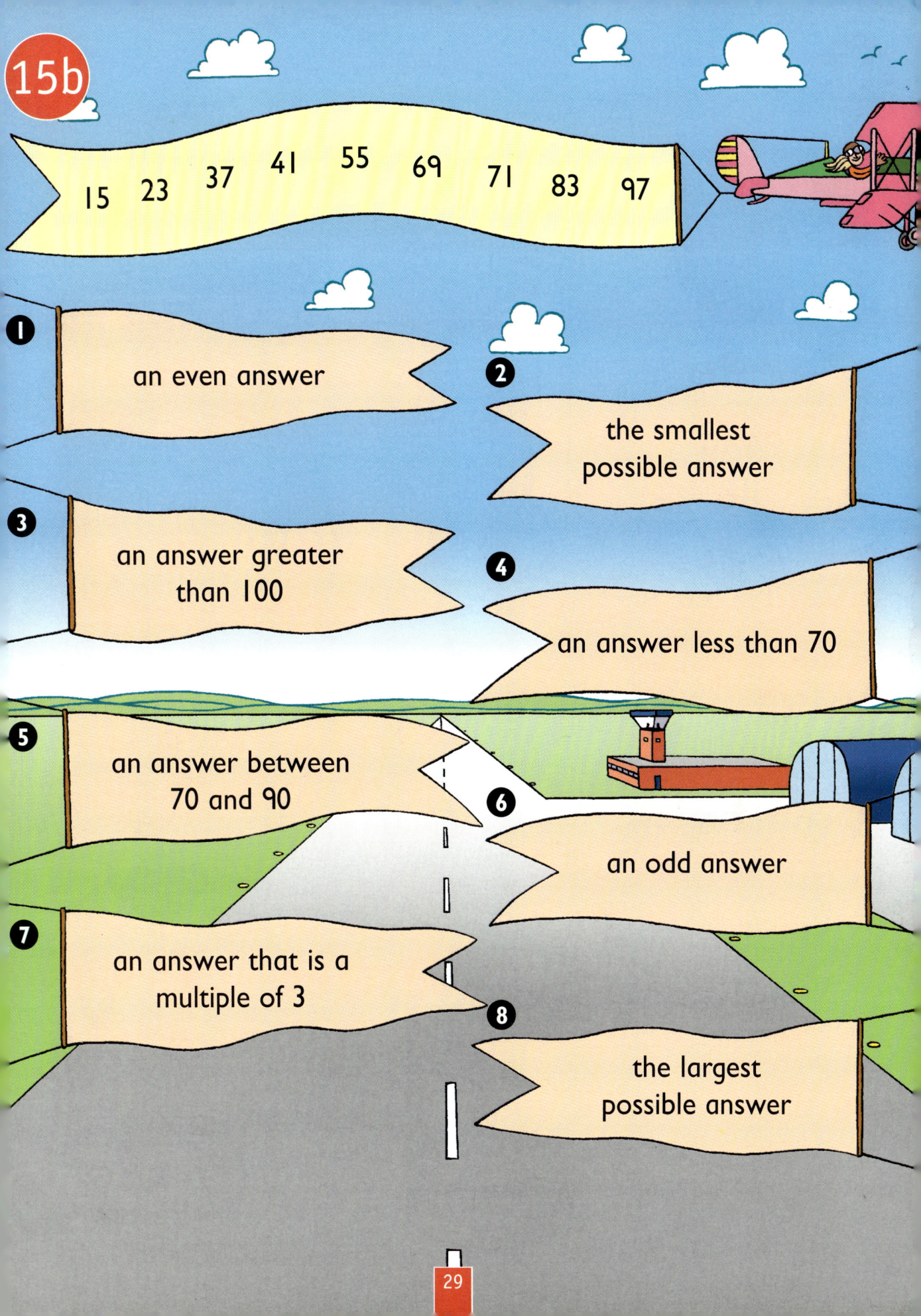

15 23 37 41 55 69 71 83 97

1 an even answer

2 the smallest possible answer

3 an answer greater than 100

4 an answer less than 70

5 an answer between 70 and 90

6 an odd answer

7 an answer that is a multiple of 3

8 the largest possible answer

16a

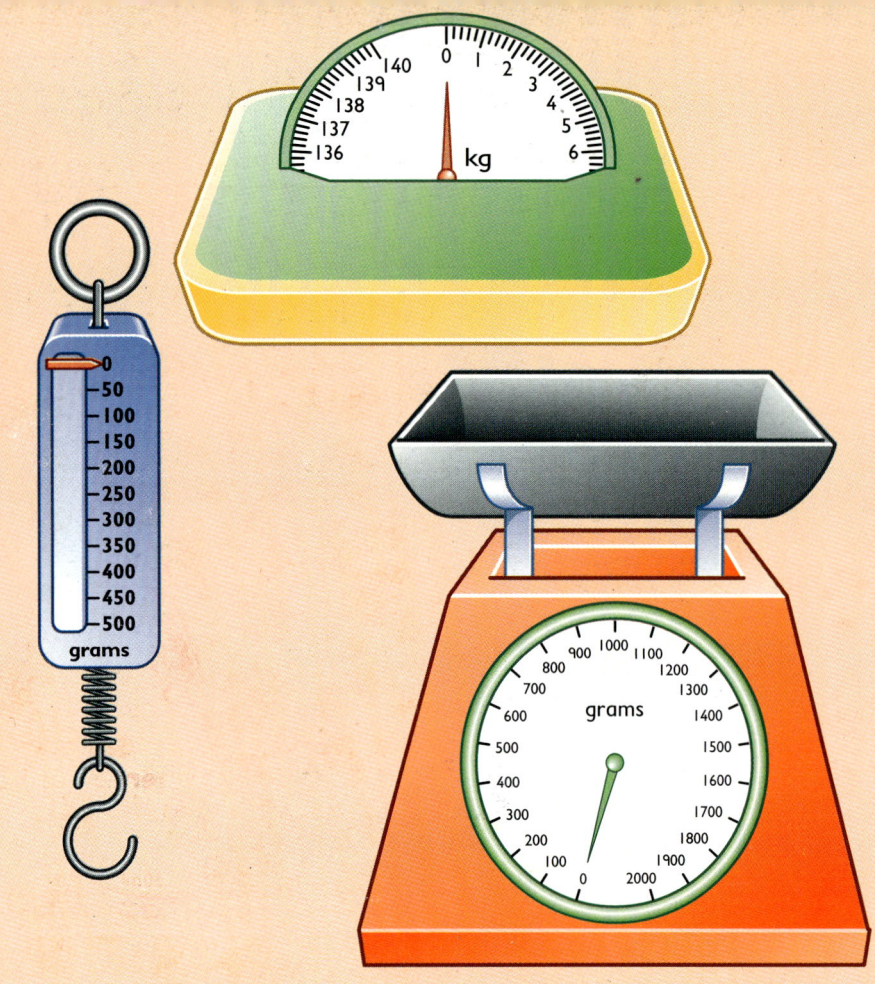

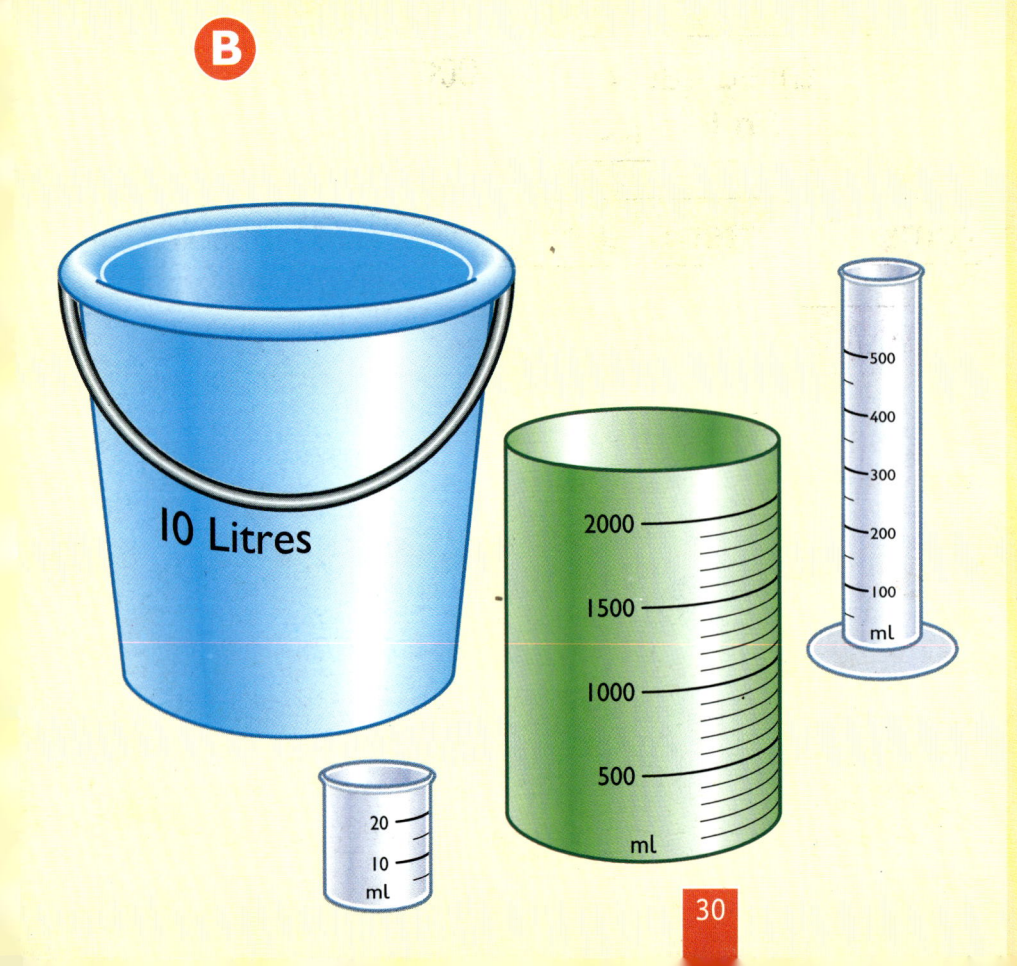

A

B

16b

A

- half a litre
- 1500 millilitres
- 5 litres
- 2 litres
- three quarters of a litre
- one tenth of a litre
- quarter of a litre
- 1000 millilitres

B

- 4000 grams
- three quarters of a kilogram
- 1000 grams
- 2 kilograms
- quarter of a kilogram
- 1500 grams
- half a kilogram
- one tenth of a kilogram

17a **A**

❶ ❷ ❸
❹ ❺ ❻

B

❶ ❷ ❸
❹ ❺ ❻

A

Prisms	number of faces	number of vertices	number of edges
Triangular prism	5	6	9
Square prism (cuboid)			
Pentagonal prism			
Hexagonal prism			

B

Pyramids	number of faces	number of vertices	number of edges
Triangular-based pyramid			
Square-based pyramid			
Pentagonal-based pyramid			
Hexagonal-based pyramid			

18 Joanna the vet keeps a record of each animal in the wildlife park.

Koala #13 F
Height . . . . 60 cm
Mass . . . . 11 kg
Expected lifespan . . . . . 17 years
Number in park . . . 14

Flying squirrel #12 M
Length (head and body) . . . . 21 cm
Mass . . . . 50 g
Expected lifespan . 10 years
Number in park 16

1 The animals visit the vet in travel boxes. A travel box has to be about twice the length of the animal when it lies down. What is a good length for each of the boxes?

2 A lorry can take two animals at a time to see the vet. What is the heaviest mass the lorry might carry? What is the lightest? Find the mass of five different pairs of animals.

Chimpanzee #3 M
Height . . . . 170 cm
Mass . . . . 80 kg
Expected lifespan . . . . 20 years
Number in park 12

Giant panda #2 F
Height . . . . 1·5 m
Mass . . . . 120 kg
Expected lifespan . . . . . 20 years
Number in park 2

Nile crocodile #4 F

Length (head to
tip of tail) . . . . 6 m

Mass . . . . 750 kg

Expected lifespan . . . . . . 100 years

Number in park. 6

Wolf #8 M

Height. . . . 65 cm

Length (head and
body) . . . 100 cm

Mass. . . . . 80 kg

Expected
lifespan . . 7 years

Number
in park 25

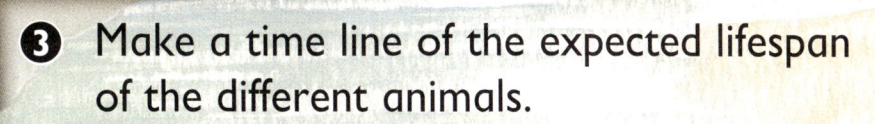

❸ Make a time line of the expected lifespan of the different animals.

❹ How many animals are there in the park altogether?

Hippopotamus #1 F

Height . . . . 1·5 m

Length . . . . 4 m

Mass. . . . . 1500 kg

Expected lifespan. . . . 45 years

Number in park 2

Lion #1 M

Height . . . . . . 91 cm

Length (head
and body) . . . . 1·5 m

Mass . . . . 200 kg

Expected
lifespan . . 24 years

Number
in park. 4

19a

Monday 1st February

Arrive by plane. **Sunny but cold at 2 °C.** Travel to catch boat. Joe attacked by polar bear.

Tuesday 2nd February

Take boat further north. Seals lying on icefloes. **Bracing wind at −2 °C.** Edgar falls down crack in ice.

Wednesday 3rd February

Travel to Base Camp on snow buggy. **Icy wind and cold at −10 °C.** Mick loses gloves.

Thursday 4th February

Arrive at Base Camp. **Cold outside at −15 °C.** Warm and snug in tent. Bert homesick and goes home.

Friday 5th February

Hitch huskies to sledge and travel north. **Five degrees colder today.** Mick gets frostbite and loses fingers.

Saturday 6th February

Blizzard. Stuck in camp. **Even cold in tent at −25 °C.** Bill lost in blizzard.

Sunday 7th February

Stumble through snow. Reach Pole. **Bitterly cold at −30 °C.** Raise flag only to find Norwegians there before us. Charlie stamps foot and breaks leg.

Monday 8th February

Not many of us left. Limp back to Base Camp. **Glad it's now −18 °C.** Charlie in a bad way and loses leg.

Tuesday 9th February

Food running out. **Snow melting at 0 °C.** Larry lost in avalanche.

Wednesday 10th February

Back at airport. **Sun shining at 5 °C.** I'm the only survivor.

Puzzle 1

Copy this diagram.
Use all the numbers 1, 2, 3, 4, 5, 6, 7, 8.
Write the numbers in the circles so that each side of the square adds up to 12.

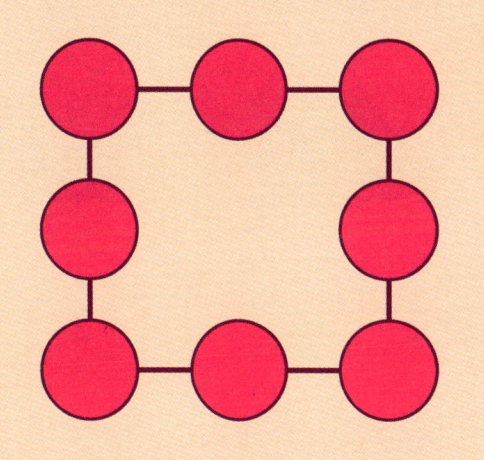

Puzzle 2

Draw three circles.
Use all the numbers 1, 2, 3, 4, 5, 6, 7, 8, and 9.
Write them in the circles so that the numbers in each circle add to 15.

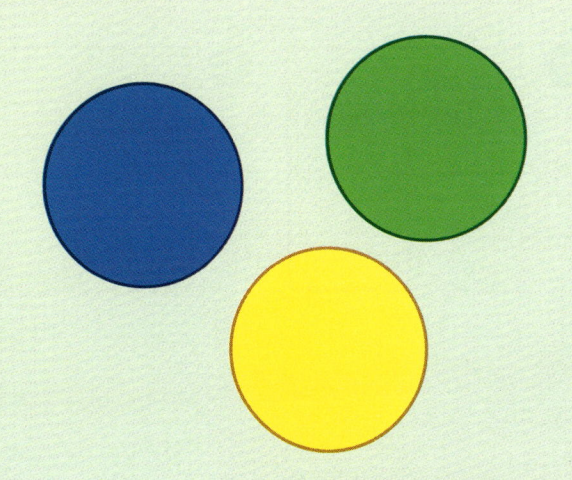

Puzzle 3

I'm thinking of a number.
I add 14.
I double it.
I subtract 8.
I halve the number.
I get 20.
What's my number?

Puzzle 4

Find a pair of numbers for each box that make the sums and products shown.

- a sum of 12
- a product of 35

- a sum of 24
- a product of 80

- a sum of 13
- a product of 42

20a

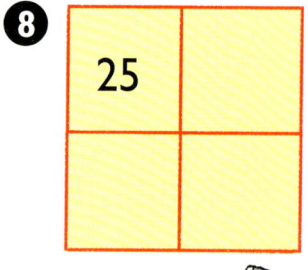

1
12	15
16	20

2
12	16
15	20

3
32	40
36	45

4
81	90
90	100

5
10	12

6
45	
50	

7
	49

8
	25

20b A

1 3 → 12 → 24   3 × 8 = 24

2 6 → ☐ → ☐   6 × 8 = ☐

3 4 → ☐ → ☐   4 × 8 = ☐

4 8 → ☐ → ☐   8 × 8 = ☐

5 7 → ☐ → ☐   7 × 8 = ☐

6 11 → ☐ → ☐   11 × 8 = ☐

7 21 → ☐ → ☐   21 × 8 = ☐

8 12 → ☐ → ☐   12 × 8 = ☐

9 25 → ☐ → ☐   25 × 8 = ☐

20b

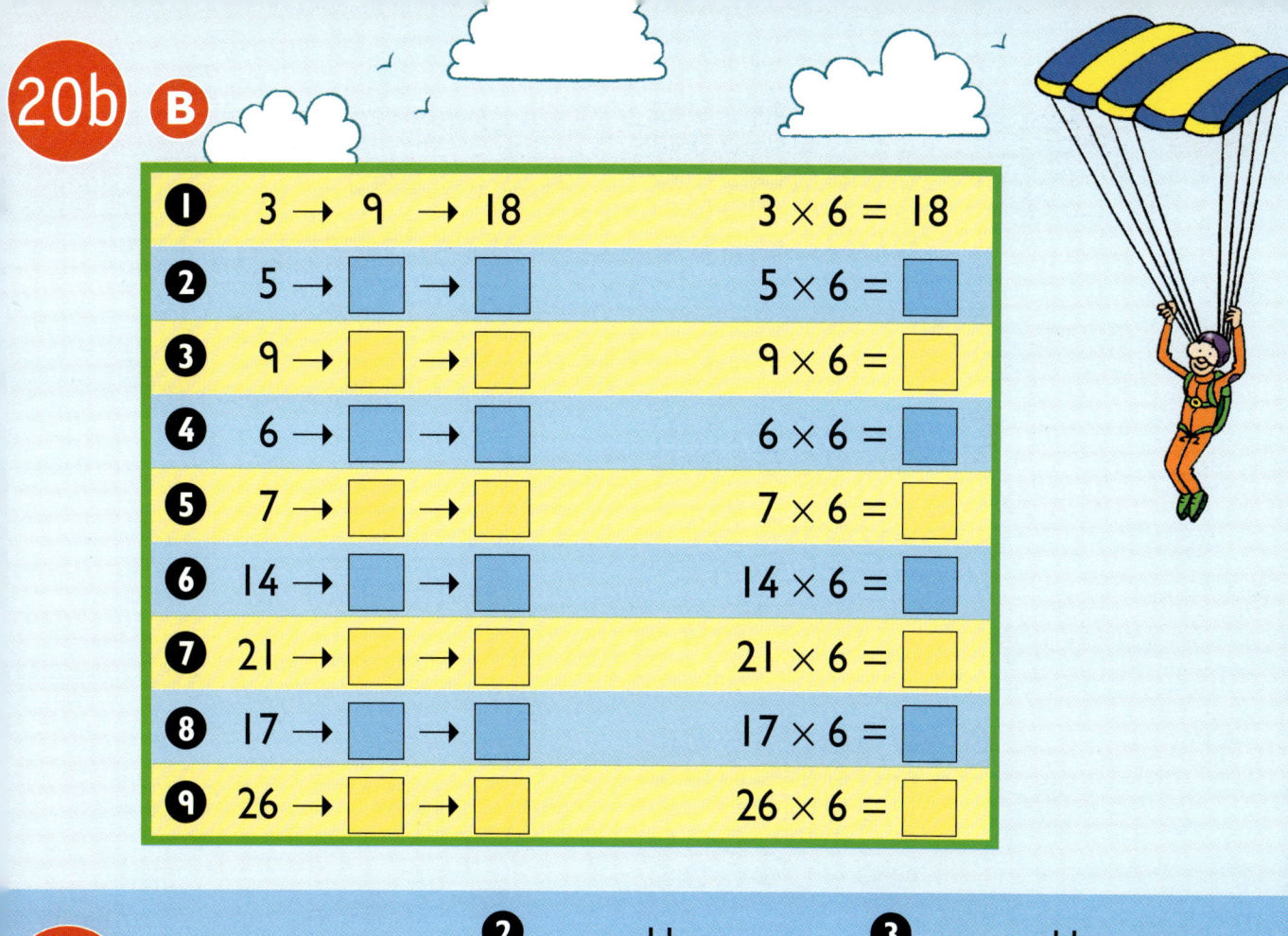

1. 3 → 9 → 18   3 × 6 = 18
2. 5 → ☐ → ☐   5 × 6 = ☐
3. 9 → ☐ → ☐   9 × 6 = ☐
4. 6 → ☐ → ☐   6 × 6 = ☐
5. 7 → ☐ → ☐   7 × 6 = ☐
6. 14 → ☐ → ☐   14 × 6 = ☐
7. 21 → ☐ → ☐   21 × 6 = ☐
8. 17 → ☐ → ☐   17 × 6 = ☐
9. 26 → ☐ → ☐   26 × 6 = ☐

20c

1. 5 × 11 = 55
2. 7 × 11 = ☐
3. ☐ × 11 = 88
4. 4 × 9 = ☐
5. ☐ × 9 = 27
6. 5 × ☐ = 45
7. 6 × ☐ = 66
8. 9 × 11 = ☐

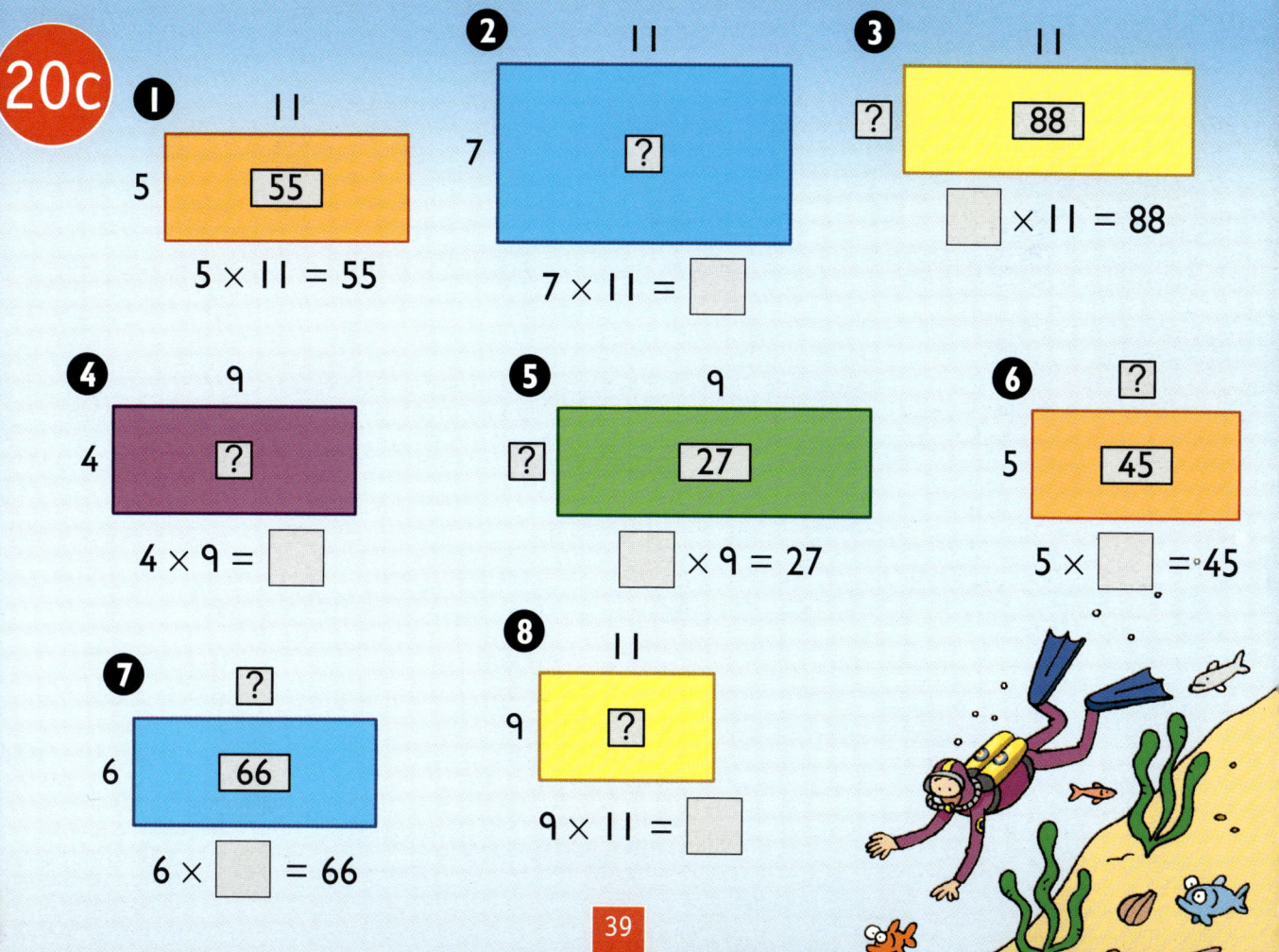

21a

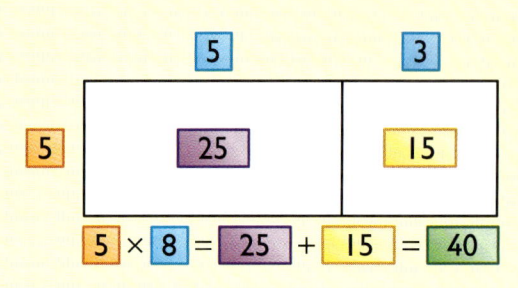

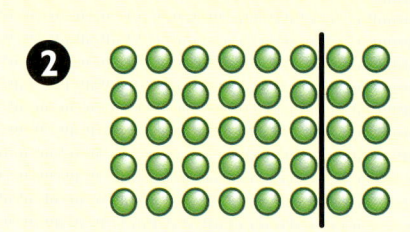

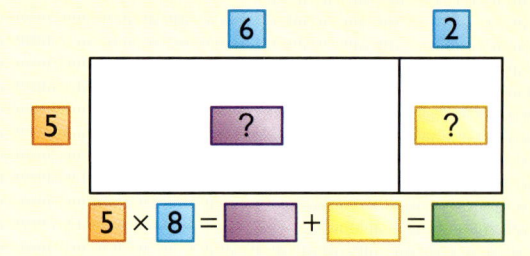

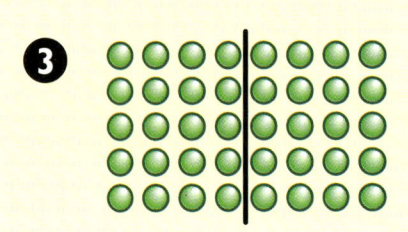

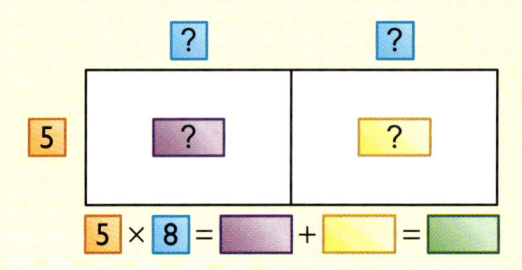

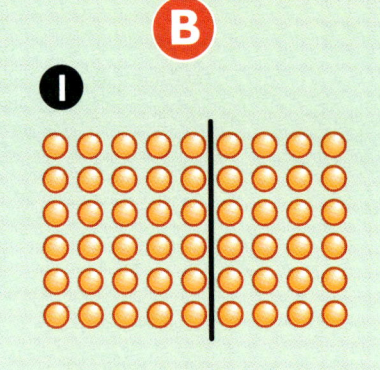

A

1. $5 \times 8 = 25 + 15 = 40$

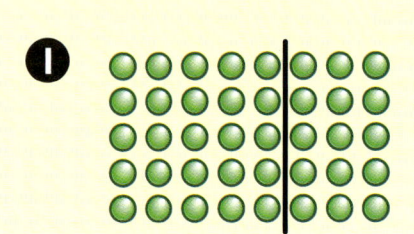

2. $5 \times 8 = \boxed{} + \boxed{} = \boxed{}$

3. $5 \times 8 = \boxed{} + \boxed{} = \boxed{}$

B

1. **2.** 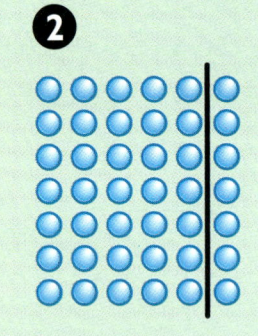 **3.** 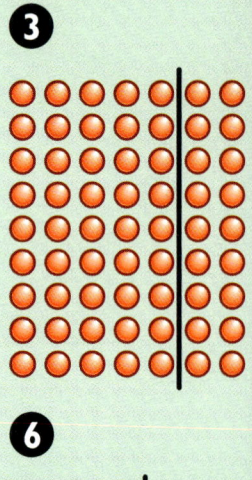 **4.** 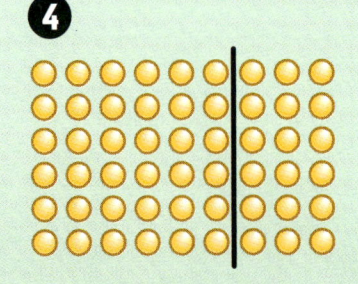 **5.** 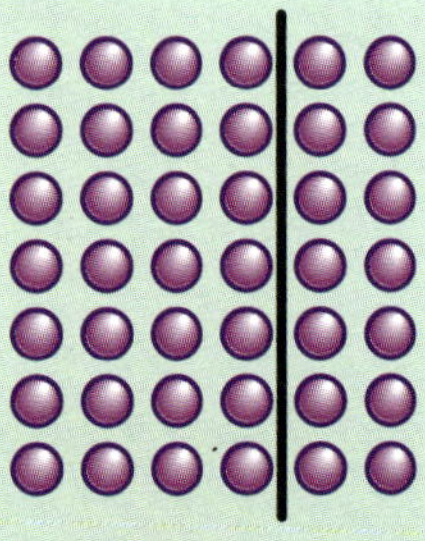 **6.**

40

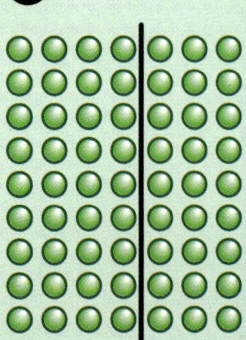

21b

A
1. 17 × 6
2. 21 × 7
3. 12 × 9
4. 24 × 5
5. 19 × 8
6. 22 × 11

B

4 6 7 8

12
22
17   24
14

Approximate answer	Calculation
60	12 × 6
40	
80	
140	
120	

21c

1. 6 × 23 Approximate: 6 × 20 = 120

```
         20      3
    6 | 120  |  18
```
6 × 23 = 120 + 18 = 138

2. 4 × 15 Approximate: _____

```
         10      5
    4 |  ?   |   ?
```
4 × 15 = ☐ + ☐ = ☐

3. 8 × 14 Approximate: _____

```
         10      4
    8 |  ?   |   ?
```
☐ × ☐ = ☐ + ☐ = ☐

4. 4 × 28 Approximate: _____

```
          ?      8
    4 |  ?   |   ?
```
☐ × ☐ = ☐ + ☐ = ☐

5. 7 × 26 Approximate: _____

```
          ?      ?
    7 |  ?   |   ?
```
☐ × ☐ = ☐ + ☐ = ☐

41

22a

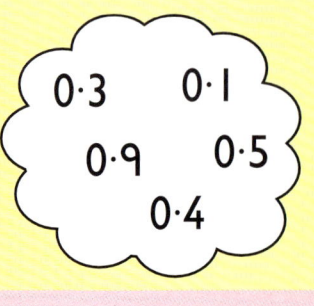

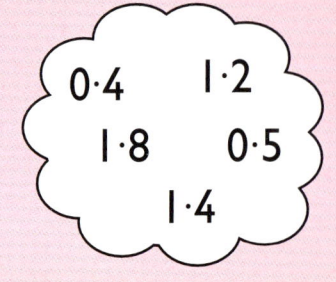

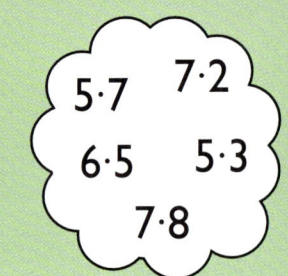

1 Number line from 0 to 1

0·3 0·1
0·9 0·5
0·4

2 Number line from 0 to 2

0·4 1·2
1·8 0·5
1·4

3 Number line from 5 to 8

5·7 7·2
6·5 5·3
7·8

22b

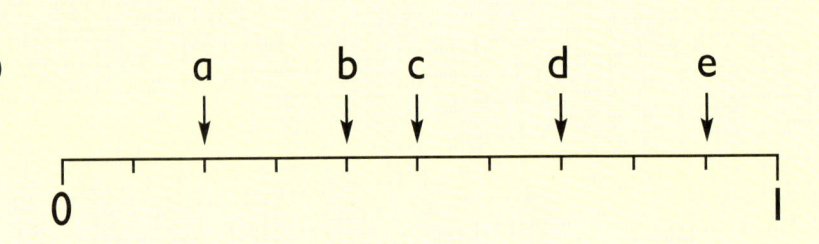

1 Number line from 0 to 1 with arrows a, b, c, d, e

2 Number line from 0 to 2 with arrows a, b, c, d, e

3   5   7   9   0·2   0·3   0·7   0·8

22c A

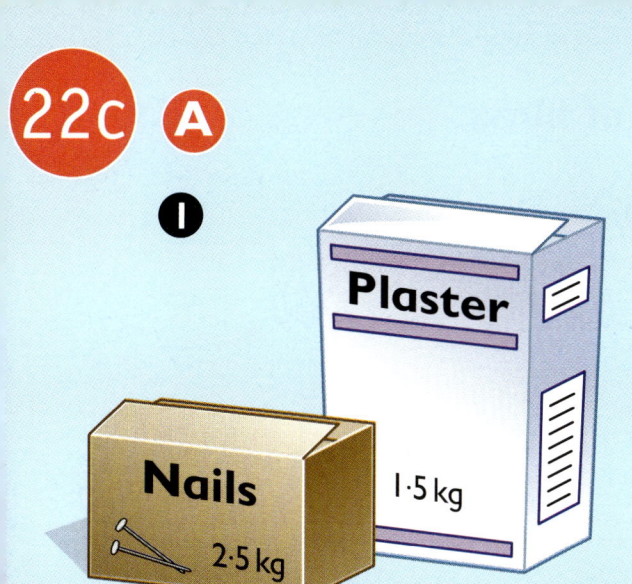

1

I think the plaster is heavier because it is a bigger box.

I think the box of nails is heavier because two point five is greater than one point five.

I think the nails weigh more, because nails are heavier than plaster.

Nails 2·5 kg
Plaster 1·5 kg

2 *I think the lemon pop and the orange pop bottles hold the same because point five is a half.*

I think there is more in the cola than the lemon pop because 25 is bigger than 5.

I think the orange pop bottle holds more than the lemon pop bottle because 1·5 litres means 1 litre and 5 millilitres.

Cola 1·25 l   Lemon Pop 1·5 l   Orange Pop 1½ l

B

1 8·3   7·5   3·8   5·7   8·5

2 6·8 m   5·8 m   8·4 m   4·6 m   6·4 m

3 8·9 kg   980 g   98 g   0·89 kg   1 kg

4 99 cm   9 m   0·9 m   1·9 m   199 cm

43

23 Jordan Hill School's survey of films

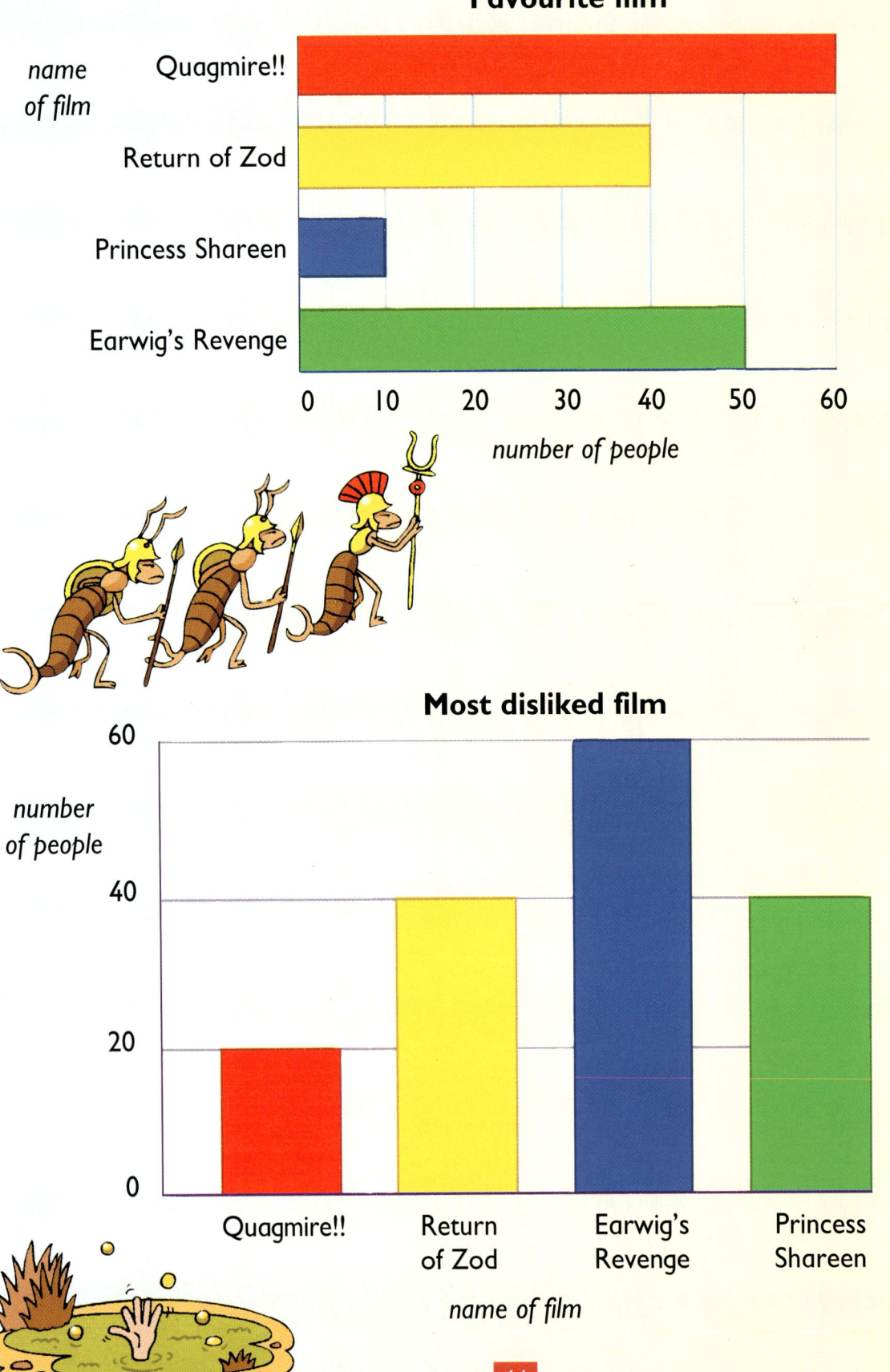

Favourite film

name of film:
- Quagmire!! — 60
- Return of Zod — 40
- Princess Shareen — 10
- Earwig's Revenge — 50

number of people

Most disliked film

- Quagmire!! — 20
- Return of Zod — 40
- Earwig's Revenge — 60
- Princess Shareen — 40

name of film

Favourite type of film

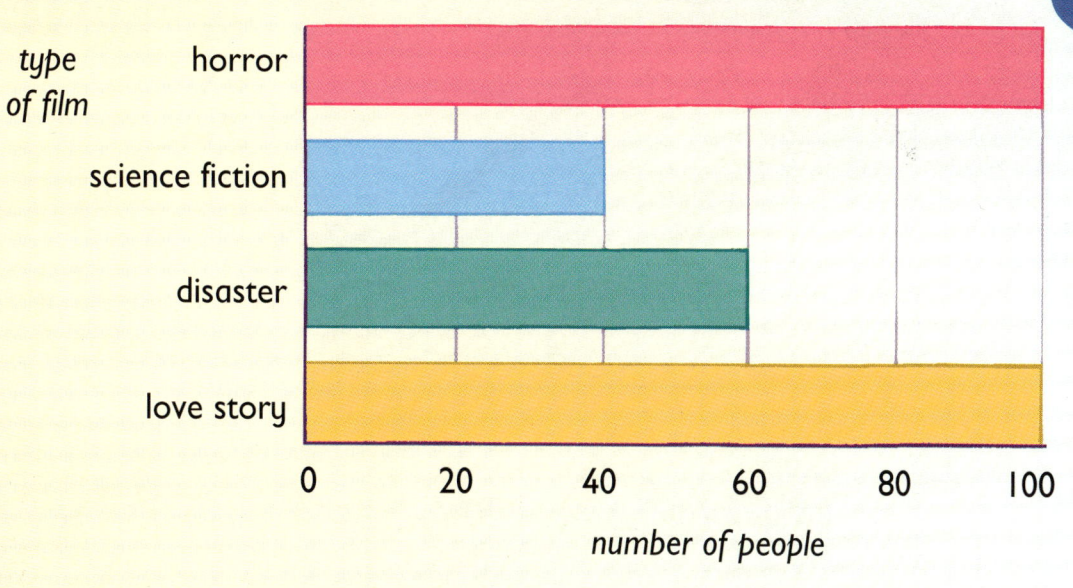

type of film	number of people
horror	100
science fiction	40
disaster	60
love story	100

number of people: 0, 20, 40, 60, 80, 100

Number of showings at JH cinema

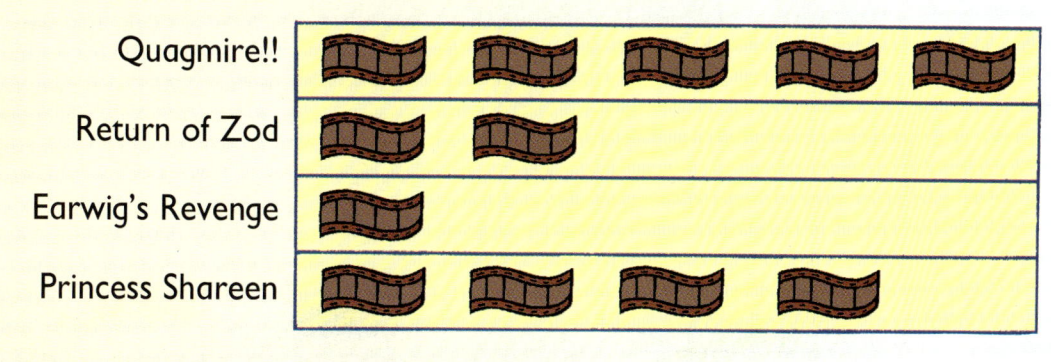

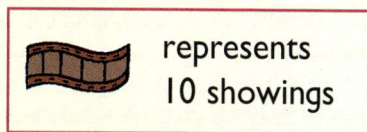

Film	Showings
Quagmire!!	🎞️🎞️🎞️🎞️🎞️
Return of Zod	🎞️🎞️
Earwig's Revenge	🎞️
Princess Shareen	🎞️🎞️🎞️🎞️

🎞️ represents 10 showings

24a

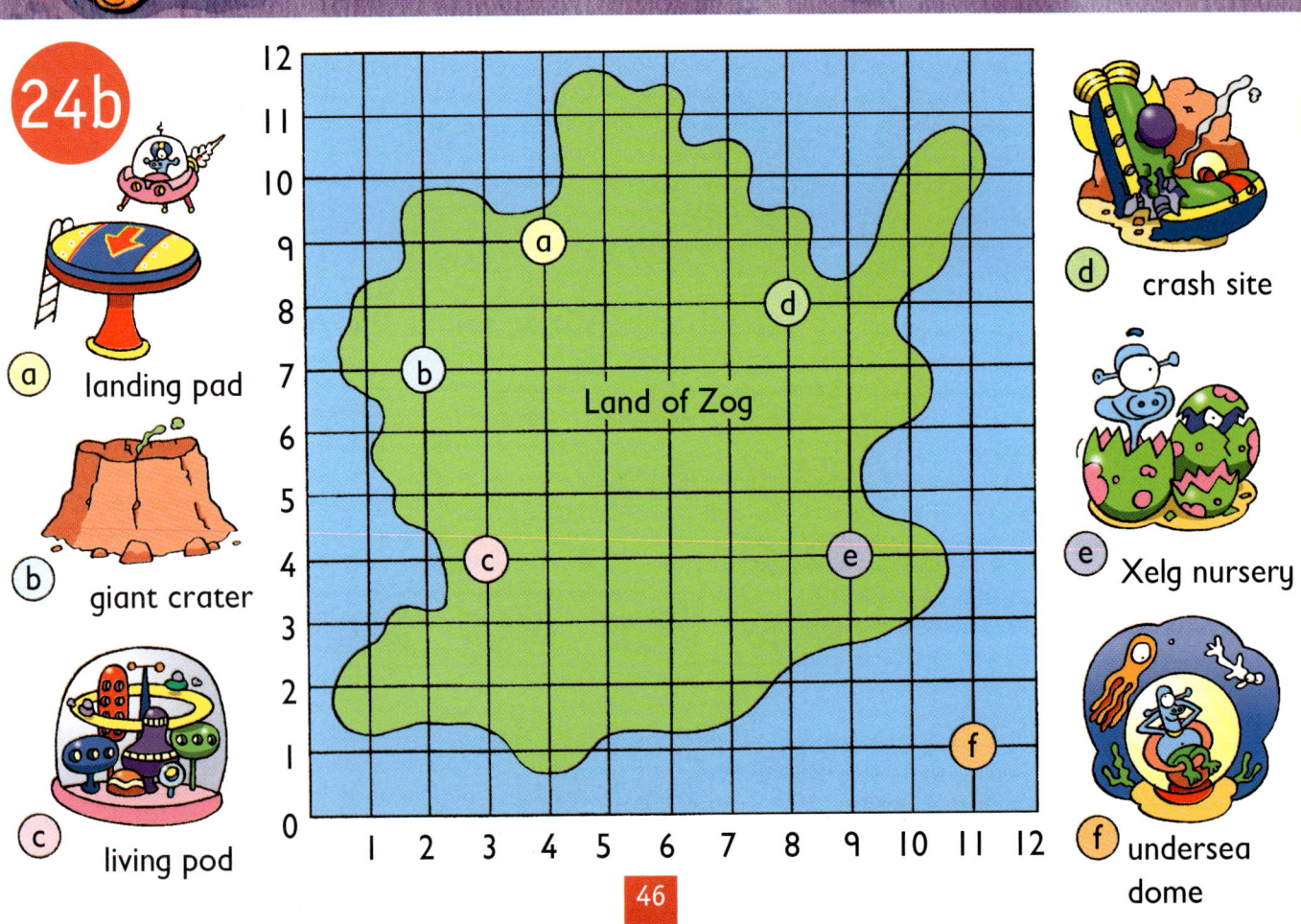

24b

- a landing pad
- b giant crater
- c living pod
- d crash site
- e Xelg nursery
- f undersea dome

Land of Zog

24c

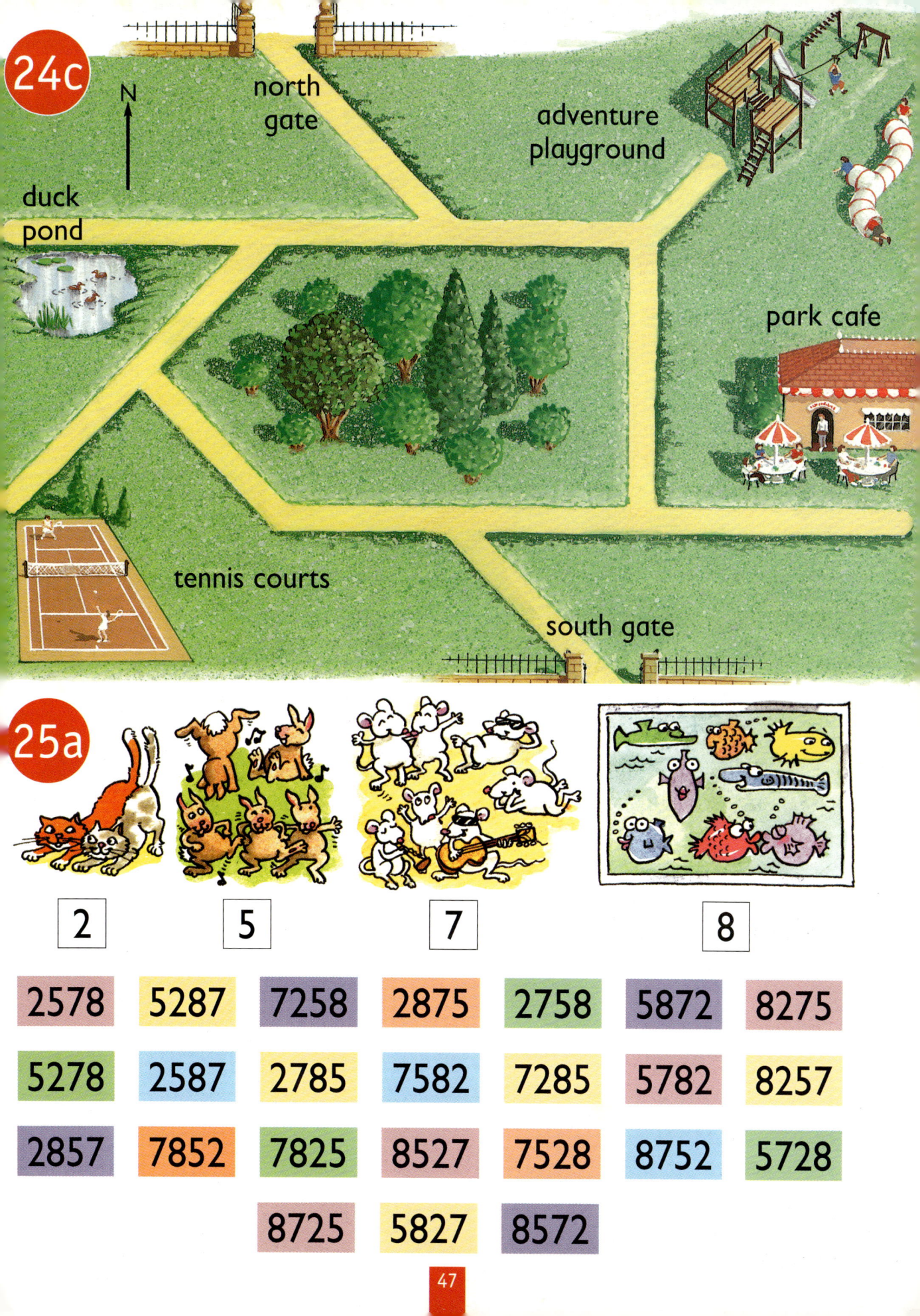

north gate

adventure playground

duck pond

park cafe

tennis courts

south gate

25a

| 2 | 5 | 7 | 8 |

2578 5287 7258 2875 2758 5872 8275

5278 2587 2785 7582 7285 5782 8257

2857 7852 7825 8527 7528 8752 5728

8725 5827 8572

47

25b BRENDA'S BARGAIN BASEMENT!

£379
£148
£203
£119
£175
£189
£227
£455
£244

714 cm
297 cm
234 cm
185 cm
104 cm

135 g
155 g
385 g
108 g
265 g
784 g

306 ml
453 ml
185 ml
855 ml
780 ml

26a

Food item	Amount left	
	day 1	day 2
raisins	49	45
peanuts	41	57
pumpkin seeds	95	97
sunflower seeds	68	74

26b

peanuts £3.45

raisins £3.49

millet 63p

sunflower seeds £4.99

pumpkin seeds £3.79

27a

499   373   560   906   800   674

39   80   68   71   86   93

27b

Four friends went shopping.
Samir had £8.55 in his pocket.
Amber's uncle gave her £7.50 to spend.
Jen had £9.63 in her purse.
Charlie took £10 out of the bank.

£4.68
£3.99
£2.00
£2.84
£1.50
£5.75

28a

1
2
3
4
5
6

28b

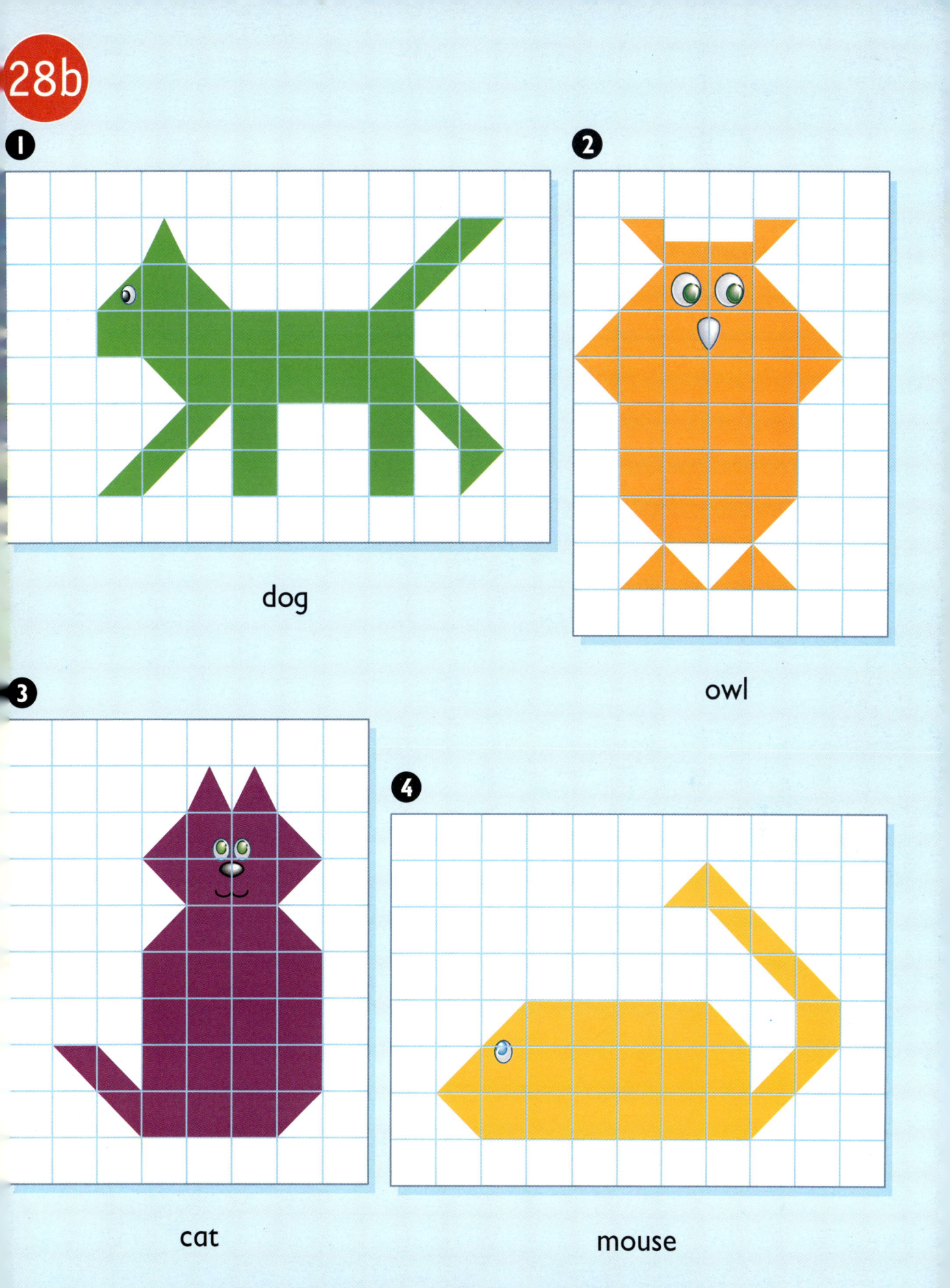

1 dog

2 owl

3 cat

4 mouse

29a

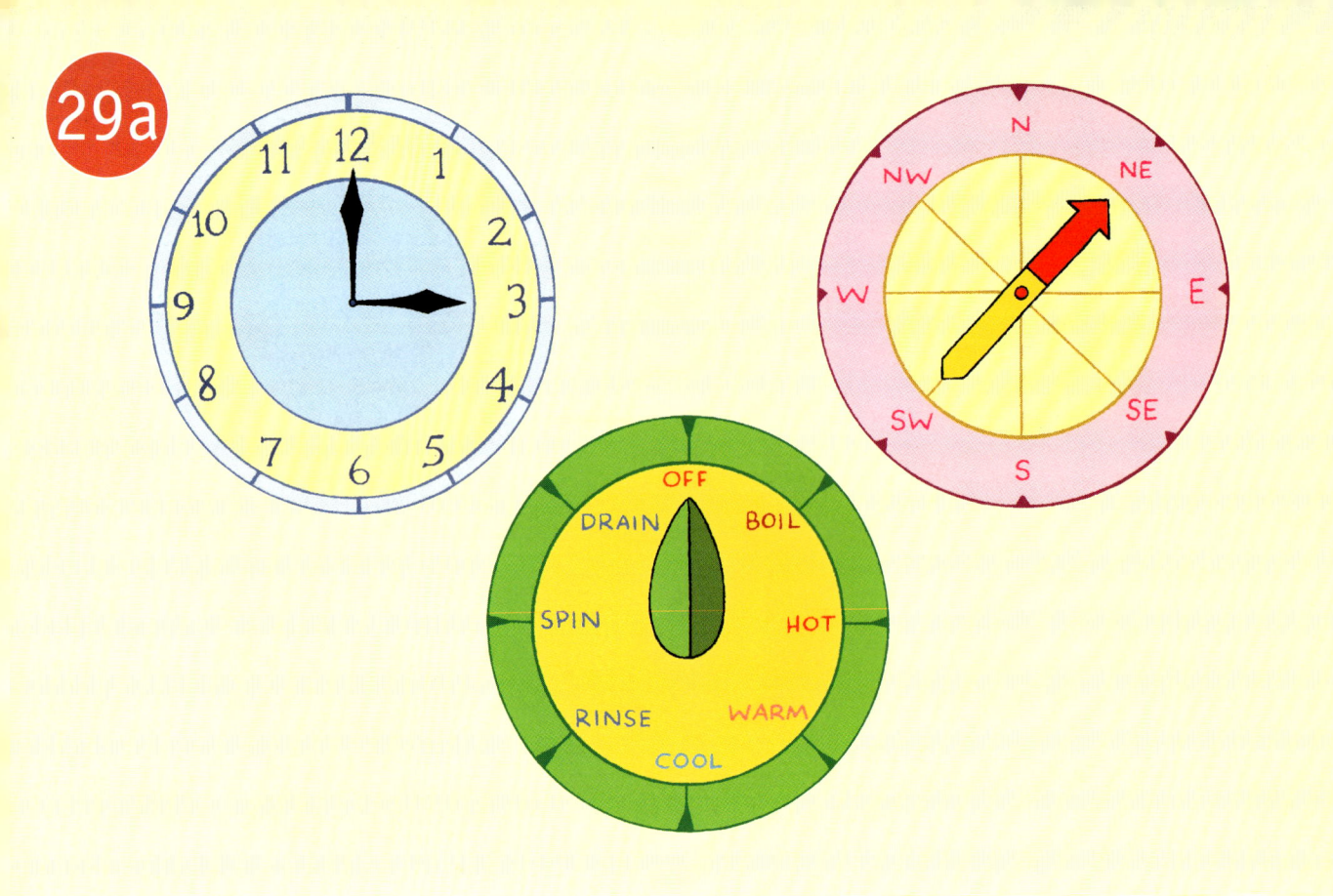

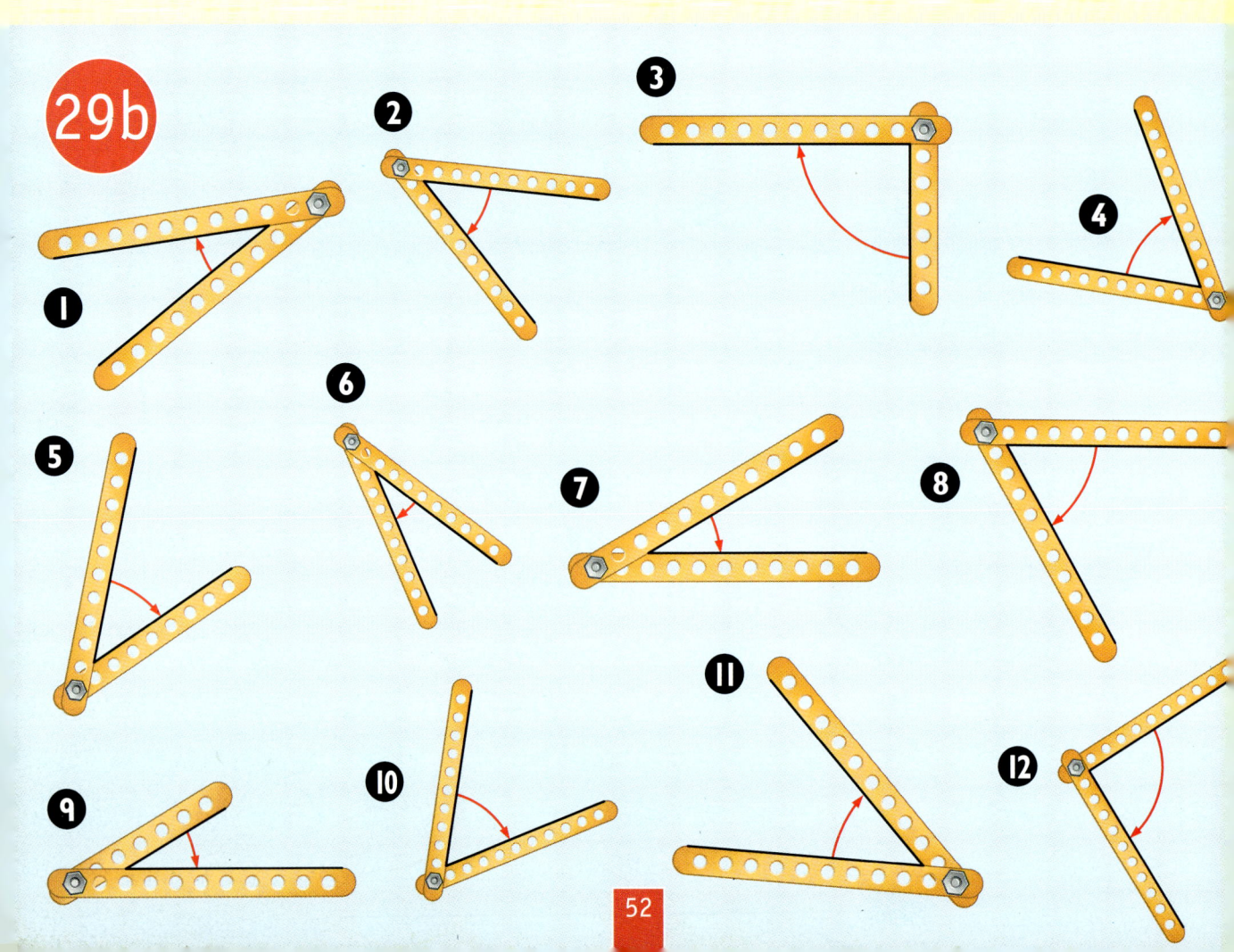

29b

30a

1) 11 / 3, 8

2) 15 / 6, 9 / 2, 4, 5

3) ___ / 4, 6

4) ___ / ___, ___ / 3, 4, 7

5) ___ / ___, ___ / ___, ___, ___ / 10, 15, 20, 25

6) 14 / 3, ___

7) 9 / 4, ___ / ___, 2, ___

8) 60 / 27, ___ / ___, 15, ___ / 5, ___, 7, ___

30b

1 Samir was sorting CDs in the music shop. There were 139 CDs in the pop section and 85 CDs in the dance music section. Samir took away 50 CDs. How many were left altogether?

2 Cherry unwrapped 3 packets of 15 CDs and one packet of 10. How many CDs did Cherry unwrap?

3 Last week the music shop sold 150 CDs and 28 T-shirts. Half the CDs sold were singles. A single costs £3 and a T-shirt costs £8.99. How many singles were sold?

4 Girl-Gang's new single is on special offer at £1.99. It sold 85 copies in one week and 79 in the next week. In two weeks Boy-Band's single sold 163 copies. Which group sold most CDs?

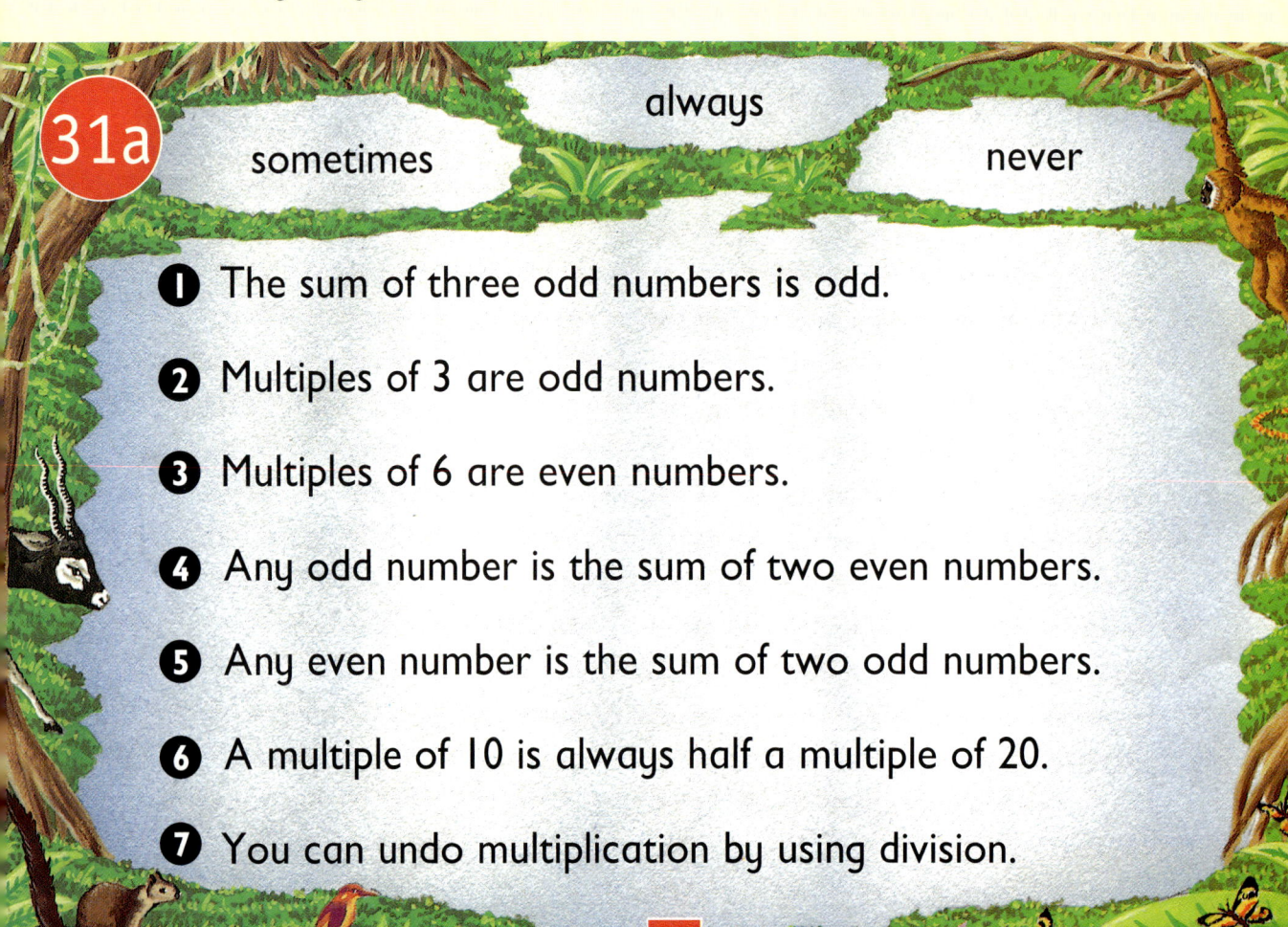

31a

sometimes   always   never

1 The sum of three odd numbers is odd.

2 Multiples of 3 are odd numbers.

3 Multiples of 6 are even numbers.

4 Any odd number is the sum of two even numbers.

5 Any even number is the sum of two odd numbers.

6 A multiple of 10 is always half a multiple of 20.

7 You can undo multiplication by using division.

31b

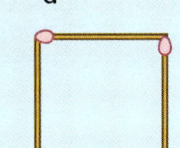

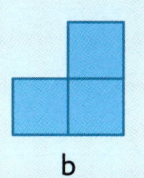

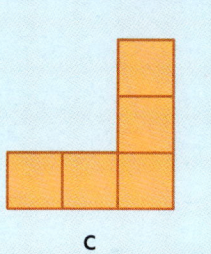

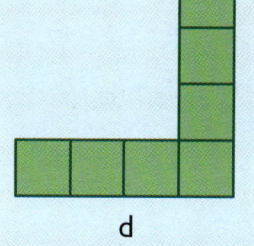

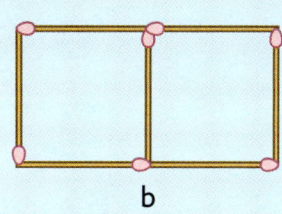

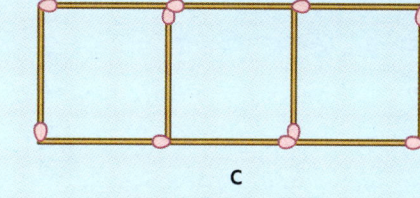

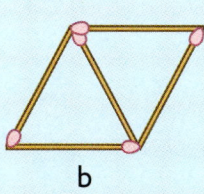

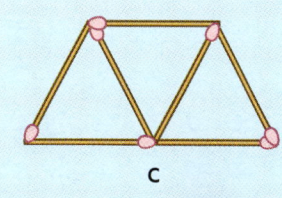

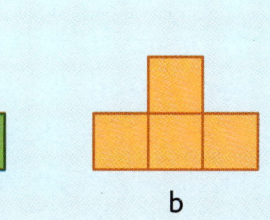

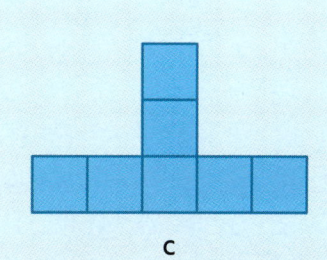

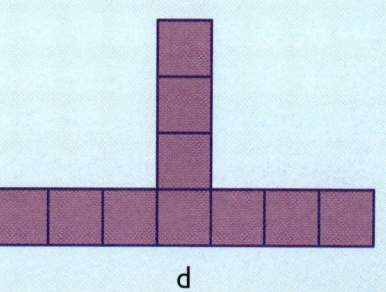

1 a, b, c, d

2 a, b, c

3 a, b, c

4 a, b, c, d

32a

❶ $7 \times 2 =$ ●

❷ $5 \times$ ● $= 15$

❸ ● $\times 4 = 32$

❹ $15 \times$ ● $= 30$

❺ $5 \times 8 =$ ●

❻ ● $\times 7 = 70$

❼ ● $\times 5 = 45$

❽ $6 \times$ ● $= 24$

❶ ● $\div 2 = 9$

❷ $24 \div 4 =$ ●

❸ $50 \div$ ● $= 10$

❹ $24 \div$ ● $= 12$

❺ ● $\div 3 = 6$

❻ $80 \div$ ● $= 8$

❼ $45 \div$ ● $= 9$

❽ ● $\div 2 = 120$

32b

❶ 26 × 3
❷ 23 × 4
❸ 19 × 6
❹ 22 × 8
❺ 18 × 5

❶ 25 × 4
❷ 17 × 8
❸ 29 × 4
❹ 18 × 3
❺ 24 × 5

32c A

❶ 35 × 11
❷ 8 × 9
❸ 2400 × 2
❹ 25 × 4
❺ 30 × 40
❻ 27 × 3

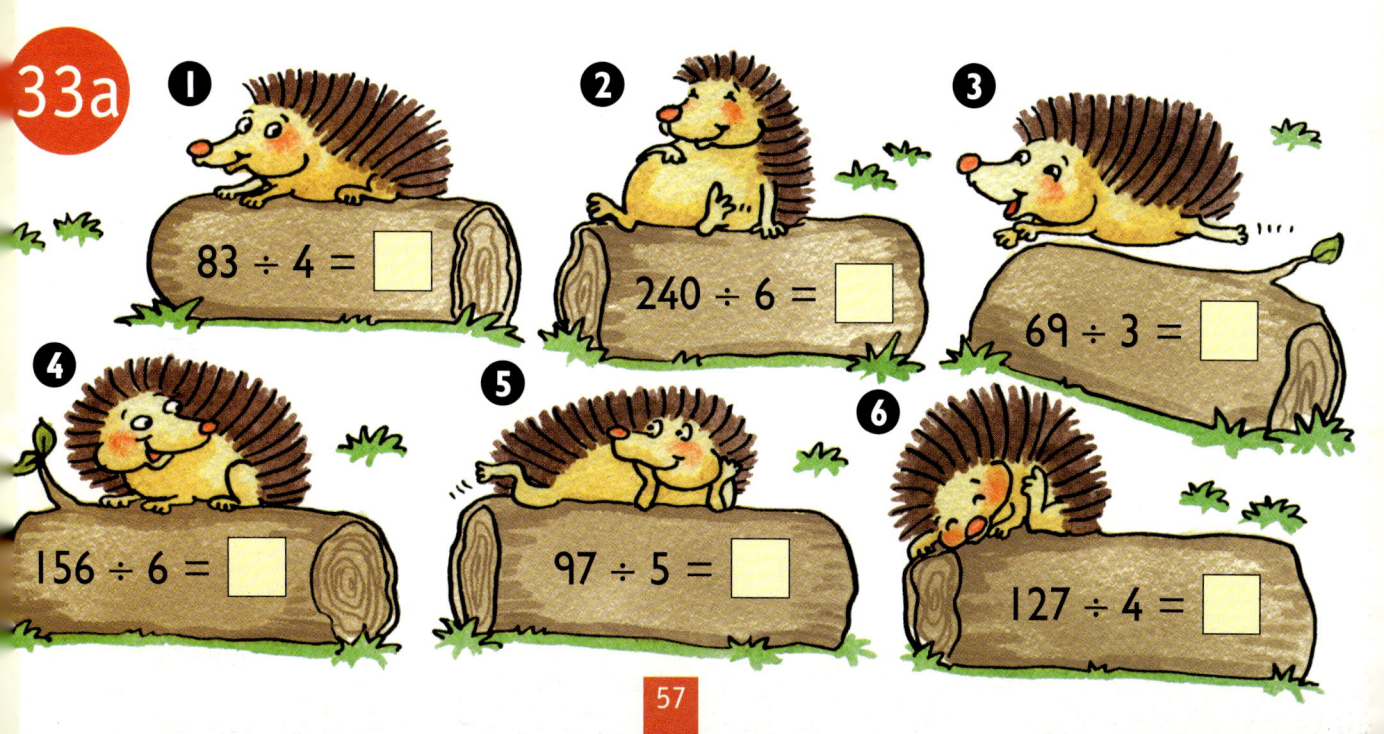

32c B

1) 25 × 5
2) 3 × 25
3) 37 × 4
4) 49 × 5
5) 10 × 76
6) 26 × 11
7) 145 × 2
8) 73 × 6
9) 33 × 3
10) 7 × 56
11) 25 × 4
12) 31 × 3
13) 38 × 4
14) 39 × 5
15) 85 × 10
16) 26 × 9
17) 132 × 2
18) 82 × 8
19) 22 × 4
20) 100 × 9

33a

1) 83 ÷ 4 = ☐
2) 240 ÷ 6 = ☐
3) 69 ÷ 3 = ☐
4) 156 ÷ 6 = ☐
5) 97 ÷ 5 = ☐
6) 127 ÷ 4 = ☐

33b

A

1. Divide £22 by 4.
2. Share £35 between 10.
3. What is £25 divided by 2?
4. What is the answer to £47 ÷ 5?
5. Divide £43 by 4.

B

1. Mrs Brassica has 62 apples. She puts 8 apples in each bag. How many bags does she fill?

2. Peaches arrive at the shop wrapped in packets of 8. Mrs Brassica unwraps the packets to sell the peaches. One day she sold 62 peaches. How many packets did she unwrap?

3. Mrs Brassica has 83 lemons and 95 oranges. She puts the lemons on trays. Each tray holds 6 lemons. How many trays does she need for all the lemons?

4. Jimmy buys 4 melons and a pumpkin. The total cost of just the melons is £13. How much does each melon cost?

5. Mrs Brassica puts oranges on the shelves in rows of 7 and apples in rows of 8. There are 36 oranges in a box. How many oranges are left over from one box after Mrs Brassica has filled as many rows as possible?

34a

1
2
3
4
5
6
7
8

59

34b

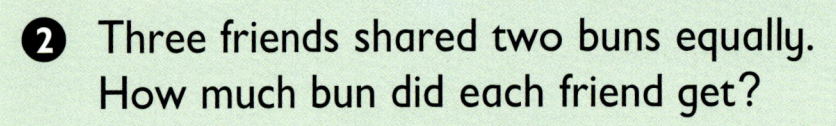

❶ Eight friends shared two bottles of cola equally. How much cola did each friend get?

❷ Three friends shared two buns equally. How much bun did each friend get?

❸ Eight friends went out for pizza. They shared twelve pizzas equally. How much pizza did each person get?

❹ Five friends shared fifteen apples. How many apples did they each get?

❺ Four friends shared ten pounds equally. How much did they each get?

35a

❶ Sam counts the budgerigars in the aviary. 17 are blue. The rest are green. There are 31 budgerigars. How many are green?

❷ Eve counts the goats. There are 24 of them. Half of them have long horns. One third of them have short horns. The rest don't have horns. How many goats have horns?

❸ The penguins are standing in 4 rows. There are 3 rows with 12 penguins each and 1 row with 4 penguins. How many penguins are there altogether?

35b

1 It costs 80p to go into the reptile house. Six children go in. Then another 3 go in. What is the total cost for them all?

2 Molly had £10 in her purse. She spent half of it on a chimpanzee T-shirt. She spent a quarter of it to name the baby chimpanzee. How much did she have left?

3 You can buy toy grasshoppers at the zoo.
Matt wants a stripy one for £3.88.
Nur wants a mottled one for £2.75.
Amy wants a plain one for £3.39.
Will £10 be enough for all three?

35c

1 The duck pond holds 300 litres of water. The bucket holds 15 litres. How many full buckets of water will it take to fill the pond?

2 There are 10 snakes in the reptile house.
1 in every 2 snakes is venomous.
How many snakes are venomous?

3 The lion enclosure is a regular hexagon. Each side of the hexagon has a fence 12 metres long. What is the perimeter of the fence?

36a TV guide for Tuesday

Channel 1	Channel 2	Channel 3	Channel 4	Channel 5
	3:30 Tennis		4:00 Crazy Gameshow	3:30 Film: Shark
4:10 Cartoon		4:00 Cat and Mouse		
4:20 Mr Jelly		4:20 Superhero	4:30 Number Quiz	
4:35 Singaround		4:45 Nature	4:55 Festival Time	
5:00 Kidznews		5:05 Down Under		5:20 News
5:10 Inventors				5:25 The Night Sky
5:33 Video		5:30 Pet Clinic	5:30 Fun With Junk	5:30 Mrs Bones
5:35 Out and About				
6:00 Newstime		6:00 Down Your Street	6:00 Kitchen Craft	6:00 News
6:30 Regional News		6:30 Evening News	6:30 Home Decorator	6:30 Sportzone
7:00 Summer Hols		7:00 Country	7:00 News	7:00 Ancient Egypt
7:30 Albert Street		7:30 Bingo!		7:30 Sea Creatures
8:00 Alien World	8:00 Film: Haunted Shack	8:00 Boys in Blue	8:00 Welsh Castles	8:00 Ambulance
8:30 Pop Hitz			8:30 Buddies	8:30 Be a Star
9:00 Interview		9:00 Gardens	9:00 Hi Fashion	9:00 Round-up

36b

A

❶ Mo and Ed went to see a film with their uncle. The film lasted 1 hour 30 minutes. The first showing started at 2:10 p.m. The second showing started 40 minutes after the end of the first.

❷ Their uncle paid £7.25 for an adult ticket and two children's tickets. The children's tickets cost £4.00 for two. Ed noticed that an over 60s ticket cost 50p less than a child's.

B SALE! PRICES SLASHED!

toy	usual price	sale price
glow-in-the-dark dots	~~65p~~	47p
wiggly snakes	~~20p~~	17p
plastic earwigs	~~60p~~	38p
clockwork teeth	~~35p~~	26p